Lifeboat!

Royal National Lifeboat Institution

Compiled and written by
Edward Wake-Walker, Heather Deane and
Georgette Purches with the assistance of the
staff of the RNLI

LONDON

IAN ALLAN LTD

Contents

First published 1989

ISBN 0 7110 1835 9

Published by Ian Allan Ltd, Shepperton, Surrey; and printed by Ian Allan Printing Ltd at their works at Coombelands in Runnymede, England

Front cover:
Another rescue — Padstow lifeboat is launched.

Back cover:
The Lifejacket — The first standard lifejacket to be issued to lifeboat crews was made of cork and came into use in 1854. It was the invention of a Capt John Ross Ward who held the post of inspector of lifeboats for 30 years. Practical but tragic proof of its effectiveness came in 1861 when Whitby's lifeboat, run in those days independently from the RNLI, overturned in huge seas while going to the aid of six ships in distress near the harbour mouth. One man on board, Henry Freeman, was wearing a Ward-designed cork lifejacket, sent to the station a few years earlier as a sample. Freeman was the only man from the crew who did not drown, almost undoubtedly because of the lifejacket he had on.

The cork lifejacket remained in vogue until 1904 when Kapok was found to be a more desirable means of providing buoyancy. Kapok is a fibrous substance obtained from plants growing in the East Indies. It was used for stuffing cushions before its buoyant qualities were discovered. After a two-year trial period, all stations were issued with Kapok lifejackets in 1906. Not only were they more durable than their cork predecessors, they were lighter, less clumsy to wear and could also support more weight for a longer time.

Today's lifejacket came into use in 1970. It is a self-righter in that it brings a man face-up in the water, it can be made extra buoyant by blowing air into it and it is fitted with a light, a whistle, a life-line and a lifting bracket.

Addenda

The 70ft 'Clyde' class and the 48ft 6in 'Oakley' class boats illustrated in *Profiles of Lifeboats in the RNLI Fleet* on the inside back cover of this book have now been withdrawn from service. Boats of the 'Mersey' class have since joined the fleet.

Clovelly Lifeboat Station has now been closed down.

Foreword

Lifeboats have changed considerably since I joined the RNLI 25 years ago. Inflatable lifeboats had only just been introduced at a handful of stations and the only all-weather lifeboat capable of more than 9kt was the prototype steel-hulled 'Waveney' class which had recently gone on service on the east coast. All other lifeboats were of conventional design, evolved and modified from the old pulling and sailing lifeboats of the previous century.

The chapters in this book which deal with the modern lifeboat fleet will show the reader just how far we have come today in modern lifeboat development. By 1993 the introduction of fast lifeboats should be complete and there will no longer be conventional wooden-hulled lifeboats in service.

It will be sad in a way to see the passing of such pleasing lines, but it would be wrong to stand in the way of progress. Lifeboats of today perform a remarkably efficient task, rescuing well over 1,000 people every year. And lifeboatmen of today, just as they have always done, deserve the best equipment the RNLI can provide. If there are chapters which show how much we have changed, there are others which demonstrate exactly how the voluntary spirit, the dedication and the courage of our crews have remained constant throughout our history. It is a proud history and I very much hope that this book, by its varied approach to the subject, will give the reader a useful insight into what is a multi-faceted and fascinating organisation.

Brian Miles, Director

Bridlington

PROFILE OF A LIFEBOAT STATION

There are 204 lifeboat stations throughout Britain and Ireland and, while all are typical, each is unique in its location, history and personalities. Although there are guidelines set down by the RNLI, each lifeboat station is administered by its own locally elected committee. Men and women of outstanding quality volunteer to serve on the lifeboats and are proud to do so; many other people help in other ways, particularly in organising coffee mornings, flag days, sponsored events and other fund raising activities. The strength and success of the lifeboat service can be attributed to the support each lifeboat receives from the local community. Quite often the lifeboat is at the very heart of the town, as it is at Bridlington.

Clean as a new pin, with miles of sandy beaches, family entertainment and generous helpings of Yorkshire fare, Bridlington is a favourite northeastern seaside resort. All through the summer, it thrives on the coachloads of trippers which invade the town every weekend, as well as the families who return each year to fill the hotels and guesthouses. Out of season, retired people enjoy the bracing cliff walks and use Bridlington as a base to explore the nearby Yorkshire moors.

Fishing is still an important industry in Bridlington, but much less so than it was at the beginning of the 19th century when it was the lifeblood of the town, responsible for Bridlington Quay's flourishing success as a port. It was this success which began Bridlington's lifeboat tradition. Bridlington Bay extends from Flamborough Head in the north to the Humber in the south. While it provides a safe haven for shipping when gales blow from north or west, the south or east winds can transform the bay into a dangerous trap, whipping up the surf on the Smithic Sands south of Flamborough Head into a seething cauldron. In the early 1800s, vessels often set out on long journeys, never to be seen again, while others sailing near the coast were frequently wrecked within sight of land, onlookers on the shore being powerless to help.

In 1806, 18 years before Sir William Hillary founded the RNLI, the townspeople of Bridlington Quay donated £300 for a lifeboat and boathouse. The boat was built by Henry Greathead, famous builder of *The Original* (see page 45), the first boat to be built as a lifeboat in 1789. There was little doubt that the boat was needed, for shortly after she began her rescue work manned by volunteer fishermen, the *East Riding Gazette* wrote: 'The vessel sacred to humanity has become an indispensable requisite, the beneficiary effects of which are experienced every season.'

Nowadays the type of rescue work has

Above:
Fred Walkington is 42 years old and very fit. He works as an electrical assembler for an engineering company and is a typical hardworking family man. Yet there is something which sets Fred apart from most other men. He is one of only 130 lifeboat coxswains in the whole of the United Kingdom and Republic of Ireland. Fred is coxswain of the Bridlington lifeboat.

Left:
Even before Fred left school, the harbour was his playground. By 15, he was a boathand. It is his natural skill and ability as a seaman, as well as his knowledge and experience of the North Sea and the northeast coast, which qualify him for the job of lifeboat Coxswain and earn him the respect and trust of the crew.

Right:
A room in Fred's house is given over to the many lifeboat bravery awards he has won, and his extensive collection of historic postcards and photographs. His father, lifeboathouse attendant for over 30 years, fostered Fred's early interest in the old Bridlington Quay Port. *Andrew Barrett*

changed at Bridlington, modern lifeboats have evolved and not so many of the crew are fishermen. In essence though, the lifeboat tradition is the same, and those involved in today's lifeboat station at Bridlington are proud of its past history and proud to be continuing the vital work.

One of the most fearful tragedies in Bridlington's history took place on 10 February 1871. No one could remember a worse gale. It claimed 70 lives and wrecked 30 ships. The two lifeboats then operating at Bridlington went out time and time again to rescue survivors; their crews were exhausted, with hands raw and bleeding from the strain of rowing. Apart from the RNLI's lifeboat — the 33ft, 10-oared, self-righting *Robert Whitworth* — a smaller boat, *Harbinger*, had been given to the fishermen by a Hungarian nobleman, Count Batthyany, who lived in the town. He had commissioned a local builder to provide the 27ft craft, which the fishermen preferred to the RNLI lifeboat. Sadly *Harbinger* was struck by a massive wave during the gale, and six of her crew of nine were lost. Still known locally as the 'Tenth of February Gale', a memorial service continues to be held annually on Fisherman's Sunday and is attended by members of the lifeboat crew.

RNLI officials met the committee and crew members after the disaster to discuss what type of lifeboat was best suited to local conditions, for although *Robert Whitworth* had performed well during the gale, the crew, with their knowledge and experience, were not happy with the lifeboat. As a result, a new 34ft self-righting lifeboat, *John Abbot*, came into service at Bridlington in August 1871. She was lighter and sharper in the bows than her predecessor giving her a greater chance of being rowed against wind and heavy sea from an open beach. The lifeboat, which also had the latest design of launching carriage, was hauled from the boathouse by six horses. She remained at Bridlington for 14 years. Three more pulling and

Below:
The men of the Bridlington lifeboats — Coxswain Fred Walkington (far right, big lifeboat), his crew members, tractor drivers and launchers. Chairman Dr Terry Wilson, and Honorary Secretary, Tony Edwards, are front row, far right and next right respectively. *Andrew Barrett*

Above:
On flat, sandy beaches, the lifeboat has to be launched into the sea by means of a tractor pushing a trailer. Bridlington is one of 22 stations which use this method. Here, *William Henry and Mary King* is recovered by tractor. *Andrew Barrett*

sailing lifeboats served at Bridlington before the first motor lifeboat, the self-righting *Stanhope Smart*, was allocated to the station in June 1931. Thousands of cheering people were there to greet the 35ft 6in lifeboat, which was powered by a 35bhp petrol engine and had a speed of 7½kt. She needed eight crew, was towed by tractor and carriage for beach launching, and cost nearly £4,000 — £3,000 more than her predecessor! *Stanhope Smart* was at Bridlington for 16 years, which included World War 2.

When the Duchess of Kent, President of the RNLI, named the next lifeboat at Bridlington, she said:

'. . . this is the first time I have named a lifeboat and I am particularly pleased that it should be at Bridlington, about which I have heard so much, and where the Institution receives such splendid support from the inhabitants, and also from the Ladies' Lifeboat Guild of the East Riding of Yorkshire. Now I have great pleasure in

Below:
The 16ft (4.34m) 'D' class inflatable lifeboat is on station between March and October and answers an average of 40 calls a year. *Andrew Barrett*

Right:
In the crew room, above the lifeboathouse, each member's gear is tidily stored, ready for the next emergency. *Andrew Barrett*

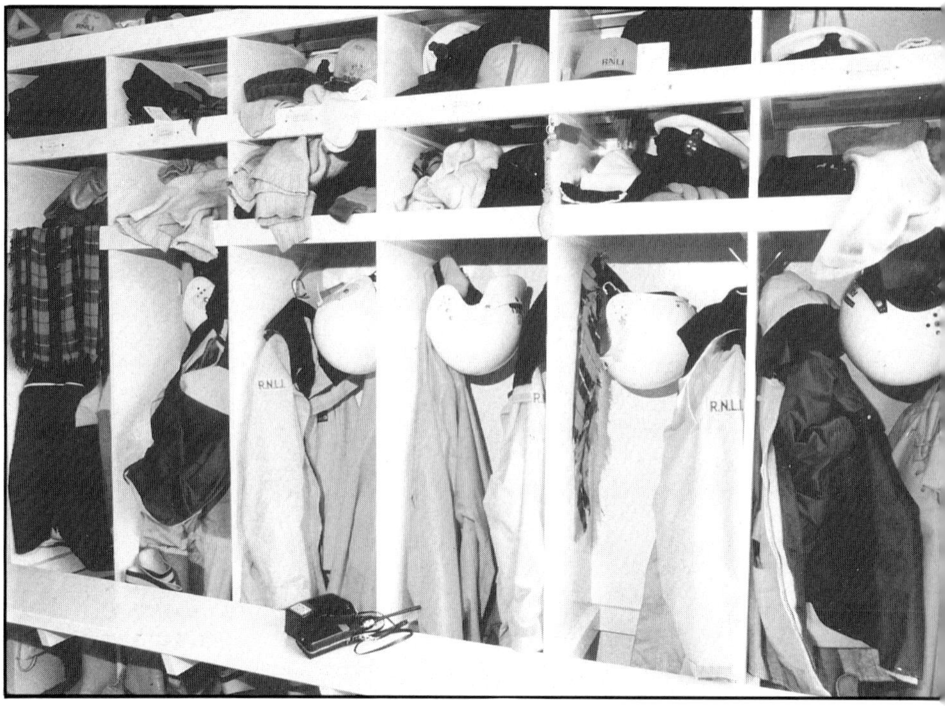

naming this lifeboat "Tilly Morrison, Sheffield".'

The most outstanding feature of the 35ft 6in lifeboat was her twin 18bhp petrol motors giving her an operational radius of 70nm and, for the first time, there was no need to carry a full complement of sails as a means of propulsion. In rough weather *Tilly Morrison* could carry 30 survivors, and her equipment included mechanical loud hailer, radio telephone, searchlight, deck light and a rocket line-throwing pistol. A small shelter, extending from the engine main canopy, was built on the deck to give protection to some of the crew. In August 1952 the lifeboat capsized in rough seas off Flamborough while going to the rescue of two girl bathers. Bowman Robert Redhead was drowned and a plaque to his memory is displayed in the lifeboathouse. While the lifeboat was away having repairs, Bridlington received a temporary 'Liverpool' class, non-self-righting lifeboat, which the crew preferred. Subsequently, in June 1953, *Tilly Morrison, Sheffield II*, a 35ft 6in 'Liverpool' class lifeboat, arrived at Bridlington. She had good shelter and was powered by twin 20bhp diesel engines giving her a speed of 7½kt and carried sufficient fuel to cover 120nm. *Tilly Morrison, Sheffield II* was at Bridlington for 14 years and was the first lifeboat there to carry out over 100 launches.

The next Bridlington lifeboat, *William Henry and Mary King*, a 37ft (11.3m) self-righting 'Oakley' class lifeboat, arrived at Bridlington on 2 September 1967. Built in 1964, she first served at Cromer, Norfolk, No 2 lifeboat station, until its closure in 1967. In her 20 years of service at Bridlington, few modifications have had to be made, the most important being the installation of radar in 1977. The lifeboat, which cost £33,000, has been launched nearly 300 times and saved over 80 lives. Many of the rescues carried out have resulted in gallantry awards for her coxswains and crew.

When the RNLI began introducing small, fast inflatable lifeboats into its fleet in the early 1960s, to cope with the growing number of people using the sea for leisure purposes, Bridlington was among the earliest stations to receive a 16ft (4.34m) 'D' class inflatable lifeboat in 1966. The lifeboat remains on station for the summer season from March to October and among the many casualties she helps are yachtsmen, windsurfers, children on airbeds and bathers cut off by the tide.

Today there are 20 lifeboat crew members and three tractor drivers for Bridlington's two lifeboats. Apart from the full time mechanic, who ensures that the lifeboat is maintained in peak condition at all times, the crew are volunteers, and include engineers, a builder, butcher, joiner, sales representative and fishermen. The men are trained to crew both lifeboats by the coxswain, Fred Walkington. They are skilled boathandlers, first aiders and radio operators, and many of them have ancestors who also served Bridlington's lifeboats. For instance, Robert Redhead is the grandson of Robert Redhead who drowned in 1952, while John Taylor's grandfather was a horse driver up until the last horse launch at Bridlington in 1920 and his son, Ian, has just joined the crew of the 'D' class lifeboat.

The RNLI imposes age limits on lifeboat crew members of 45 years in the smaller lifeboats and 55 years in the larger craft. No station experiences a shortage of volunteers, despite the nature of the work involved and the small payments of £5 for the first hour at sea, and £1.70 for each subsequent hour.

Right:
The lifeboathouse for *William Henry and Mary King* is situated in the main street and the lifeboat is pulled by tractor down the road, to the beach. The 'D' class lifeboat is housed on the beach.
Andrew Barrett

William Henry and Mary King exercises once a month if she has not been called out on service, often with a helicopter from No 22 Squadron at RAF Leconfield or another lifeboat from the flanking stations of Filey, Flamborough, Withernsea and Humber. The lifeboat carries a crew of seven and the exercises ensure that the men remain fit, work well together as a team and are always prepared for a rescue situation.

The 'D' class lifeboat has a crew of two or three and will exercise twice a week during the summer if she has not been out on service. At weekends, several of the crew work shifts during the day, remaining at the lifeboathouse on the beach ready to launch immediately if someone needs help.

A committee of volunteers deals with the administration of the station, the key post being the Honorary Secretary who is usually a person with marine qualifications. The committee is guided by full time RNLI divisional staff led by Tom Nutman, Divisional Inspector of Lifeboats for the northeast, and his deputy Tim Harrison who, on their regular visits to the station, attend committee meetings, take part in lifeboat exercises and examine the lifeboat and equipment. They are the station's link with RNLI Headquarters, passing on news, requests for stores and dealing with any day-to-day problems. The Inspectors may be contacted at any time of the day or night and will go to the station immediately if necessary, for instance, if the lifeboat is

Above:
***George and Jane Walker* served at Bridlington for 33 years. This picture was taken in 1916: the last horse launch at Bridlington was in 1920**

Below:
***William Henry and Mary King* escorts a fishing boat during a storm.** *Arthur Dick*

Left:
William Henry and Mary King **is launched in rough seas to answer a distress call. The lifeboat launches an average of 30 times a year, mainly to cargo or fishing vessels. Some 60% of lifeboat call-outs are in the hours of darkness and one in seven call-outs involves sick or injured persons.**
Hull Daily Mail

Below left:
William Henry and Mary King **goes to the aid of a small trawler.**

engaged in a particularly dangerous rescue operation. When an especially meritorious service has been carried out, the inspector will write a full report to the RNLI Headquarters recommending a gallantry award which is carefully assessed and considered by the Committee of Management of the RNLI.

The Honorary Secretary records every lifeboat launch and sends details on a return of service form to RNLI Headquarters at Poole. He decides whether the lifeboat should be launched and has deputies for leave periods. Tony Edwards, a local government officer, is the 15th Honorary Secretary to serve at Bridlington. Formerly a member of the 'D' class lifeboat crew, Tony was appointed Honorary Secretary in 1986 and he encourages the warm camaraderie which exists among the crew members.

On the first Wednesday of every month they gather for a social evening at *Tilly Morrison*, named after the old lifeboat which now serves as a museum as well as a popular bar. Families of the crews are also invited to social events and become involved in fund raising, dressing up in their skilfully made and elaborate fancy dress costumes to entertain holidaymakers on harbour gala days, and organising annual sponsored snooker contests. Children of crew members are attracted at an early age to becoming crew members themselves when they reach the qualifying age of 17. Many of the crew's wives are members of the Bridlington Luncheon Club, responsible for raising over £1,000 each year, or the Ladies' Lifeboat Guild which raises up to £15,000 a year. Visitors are welcomed, either individually or in school parties or other previously booked groups, to look around the lifeboat house; there is no better publicity for the RNLI than the sight of an immaculately kept lifeboat and tractor with display boards, photographs and posters relating to the history and work of the station.

Alongside, a well-stocked souvenir shop, run by super salesman Doug Grey, does a roaring trade helping the station

Right:
There has never been a worse storm in Bridlington than that which took place in February 1871, and an annual memorial service continues to be held.
Fred Walkington collection

BRIDLINGTON'S LIFEBOATS' RECORD

	LAUNCHES	LIVES SAVED
LIFEBOATS OVER 10 METRES	*590*	*319*
LIFEBOATS UNDER 10 METRES	*427*	*192*
TOTAL	**1,017**	**511**

BRIDLINGTON LIFEBOAT STATION

— *MEDAL AWARDS* —

1828	*Silver Medal*	John Usher
1834	*Silver Medal*	George Gray
1865	*Silver Medal*	Thomas Frankish
1867	*Silver Medal*	James Harrington
1890	*Silver Medal*	Henry Hutchinson
1893	*Silver Medal*	Christopher Brown · Fred Brown · Thomas Clark Richard Purvis · John Usher
1968	*Bronze Medal**	Coxswain John E. King
1972	*Bronze Second-Service Clasp*	Coxswain John E. King
1973	*Silver Medal*	Coxswain John E. King
1979	*Bronze Medal*	Coxswain Fred Walkington

* The *Bronze Medal* was instituted in 1917

branch to raise up to £30,000 each year, a staggering sum for a small town. As with all stations, money raised is sent to RNLI Headquarters to be spent or invested as required.

No one can say what persuades people to leave money to the RNLI, yet nearly two-thirds of its income comes from legacies. Miss Mildred Caird recently left £500,000 to Bridlington lifeboat station and the money is to be used towards the purchase of a new 12m (38ft) 'Mersey' class lifeboat. The £350,000 lifeboat, which arrived on station at the end of 1988, has been designed and developed entirely by RNLI staff and is the first British lifeboat to be built with an aluminium hull. She is self-righting, powered by twin 285hp Caterpillar 3208T turbocharged diesel engines, and fitted with the latest communications and navigational equipment. In order to accommodate the slightly larger new lifeboat, alterations will need to be carried out on the lifeboathouse and this has inspired even greater fund raising activities!

Bridlington was one of the stations chosen by the RNLI to carry out trials with the new design. The coxswain and crew were impressed with the lifeboat's performance, and received training both in the classroom and on their new lifeboat at RNLI Headquarters, Poole, before sailing *Alex and Peggy Caird* to her home town for a welcome in the best traditions of the people of Bridlington. Yet another phase in the station's history has begun.

Rescue!

Whether it be by oar or sail or engine; up hills, down cliffs or over beaches, the lifeboat will launch whenever, wherever it can, if there are lives at stake. Here described are some of the acts of supreme bravery and daring which have since passed into RNLI folklore.

Overland to Save Lives

One of the most famous lifeboat services occurred on 12 January 1899 when the Lynmouth lifeboat *Louisa* was hauled overland to go to the aid of a ship in distress. The storm was so fierce that the lifeboat could not be launched at Lynmouth and was pulled on her carriage, up the fearsome, one-in-four Countisbury Hill, over 10 miles of windswept Exmoor and down the equally treacherous Porlock Hill, so that she could be launched in the relative calm of Porlock Bay. Twenty horses pulled together, a wheel came off, gate posts were knocked down and lanes widened; even a cottage wall had to be demolished. The journey took 10½hr and then, unfed, cold, wet and exhausted the lifeboatmen launched the boat and rowed to the ship's assistance. The story is retold in graphic detail at the Information Centre in Lynmouth and a drive along the same route, even in present times, brings home the near impossibility of such a feat.

Seventy-five years ago, on 30 October 1914, another overland launch set the scene for one of the most exhausting rescues of all time. In the early hours of that morning the hospital ship *Rohilla*, on her way from Queensferry to Dunkirk with 229 people on board, including medical

Below:
Coxswain Michael Scales of St Peter Port, Guernsey, was awarded the Gold Medal for gallantry when he and his crew rescued 29 men from the *Bonita* in hurricane force winds on 13 December 1981. The illustration is from a painting by H. Beavis.

Left:
Four years after the historic 1899 overland launch, Lynmouth lifeboat *Louisa* is hauled through the town for another more conventional launching.
T. Toyne/Jerome Dessain & Co

staff and five nurses, was driven ashore at Saltwick Nab near Whitby, Yorkshire, in a tremendous southeasterly gale.

Whitby had two pulling lifeboats but there was no hope in the terrible weather of launching No 1. Thomas Langlands, the Coxswain, resolved to launch No 2 moored in the haven, but to get her to sea with the wind as it was would mean an overland journey. So it was that the boat was hauled manually, on skids, from the east pier until she was near the wreck. The task was grim and before she reached the water's edge she had been holed in two places.

Undeterred, Langlands and his crew launched — an achievement in itself — and reached the wreck, taking off 12 men and all five nurses. Despite the conditions the lifeboat put out again and although the crew found it almost impossible to reach the *Rohilla*, a quarter-of-a-mile offshore, they succeeded, and in spite of huge seas breaking over the steamer and filling the lifeboat, 18 men were taken off. The return to shore was terrifying but Langlands managed to beach the badly damaged lifeboat. She was now too damaged to continue.

So it was that a second overland launch took place. The people of Upgang, just to the west of Whitby, brought their lifeboat overland, horse-drawn, and lowered her down the cliffs by rope. By the time she was ready to launch the gale had worsened and the crew knew they would stand no chance. They waited all night and even next morning when they were able to make an attempt at rescue, the seas and strong current forced them to return without even reaching the wreck. Seeing the Upgang lifeboat approach, some men from the *Rohilla* jumped into the sea in an effort to reach her. Several were drowned but a few, helped by onlookers who dashed into the surf, were brought ashore exhausted.

By this time other lifeboat stations had been contacted by telephone. Both the Scarborough and Teesmouth lifeboats put out. The Scarborough boat, towed to sea by the steam trawler *Morning Star*, arrived at 6pm and stood by for hours in dreadful weather. All her attempts to reach the wreck failed and eventually she was forced to return. The Teesmouth lifeboat was towed by the Harbour Commissioner's tug but she sprang a leak and the crew had to abandon her. Thomas Langlands managed at last to launch the Whitby No 1 lifeboat but he still could not reach the wreck.

At last modern technology came to the aid of the *Rohilla*. The motor lifeboat at Tynemouth launched and through the raging sea, and in total darkness with all coastal lights extinguished, the lifeboat made the 44-mile journey to the scene. She arrived at 1am on Sunday 1 November. Her Coxswain was Robert Smith. With him was Capt H. E. Burton of the Royal Engineers, the Honorary Superintendent of the Tynemouth station. Smith took on board Cdr Basil Hall who was at Whitby to co-ordinate the rescue efforts.

All Whitby turned out to witness the rescue. At daybreak the lifeboat came within 200yd of the wreck and it seemed as if she too had been defeated. However, gallons of oil were then released and as reported in the *Yorkshire Post*: '. . . the lifeboat turned about, raced at full speed outside the line of breakers, past the stern of the wreck, and then turned directly towards the shore. The most dangerous moment came when she was inside the surf and broadside on to the waves; but, guided with splendid skill and courage, she moved forward steadily, and a cheer of relief went out from the shore when she reached the lee of the wreck, immediately beneath the crowded bridge. The feelings of those on board as they saw salvation at hand can only be imagined.'

There were still 50 men on board the *Rohilla* but within a quarter-of-an-hour more than 40 had been taken off. Suddenly, two huge waves swept over the lifeboat and she disappeared. After a moment of terrible suspense, she reappeared, went once more alongside and rescued the rest. The Captain was last to leave, wearing an overcoat and *pince-nez*, apparently quite unruffled.

For this exceptional rescue Gold Medals were awarded to Coxswain Smith and Capt Burton of Tynemouth, and Thomas Langlands of Whitby. Silver Medals were awarded to Cdr Hall, Richard Eglon, Langlands' assistant, James Brownlee of Tynemouth and to George Peat who had been foremost among those who had dashed into the sea to save the survivors who had tried to swim from the wreck. The Upgang crew received the RNLI's thanks inscribed on vellum for their gallant attempt.

Motorpower had proved itself over manpower, but the endurance and persistence of lifeboatmen remained the all-important element.

Gold Medal Service

December 1981 was a momentous month for the RNLI. Few people are likely to forget the tragedy which befell Penlee lifeboat on the night of 18 December when her entire crew of eight were lost, together with the eight they were trying to save from

the motor vessel *Union Star* in one of the worst storms to hit Cornwall for many years. Much has been written about the events of that night and the heroism of the lifeboat crew whose deeds were recognised by the posthumous award of the Gold Medal to Coxswain Trevelyan Richards and Bronze Medals to the rest of the crew.

No Gold Medal has been awarded since that date, so rare is the honour. It is all the more remarkable then that only five days earlier another Gold Medal service took place when Guernsey's St Peter Port lifeboat survived a hurricane to rescue 29 people from a sinking merchant vessel in mid-Channel.

Above:
Whitby, 30 October 1914: the wreck of the hospital ship *Rohilla* lies behind Whitby's pulling lifeboat which was damaged while carrying out two separate rescues. Pulling lifeboats from neighbouring stations were called but it was Tynemouth's new motor lifeboat which eventually reached the scene and was able to rescue the remaining survivors.

DISASTERS

Lifeboat disasters are rare because lifeboats are designed to withstand the very worst conditions, and on occasions in recent years the self-righting capability of lifeboats has prevented serious loss of life. However, the sea is an awesome enemy and has claimed the lives of 435 lifeboatmen since the foundation of the RNLI in 1824. The loss of one man is of course a tragedy but there have been disasters which claimed whole crews. Some of the worst losses of life are listed below:

1880	WELLS	*Eleven*	*Two survivors*
1886	ST ANNES	*Thirteen*	*No survivors*
1886	SOUTHPORT	*Fourteen*	*Two survivors*
1895	DUN LAOGHAIRE	*Fifteen*	*No survivors*
1916	SALCOMBE	*Thirteen*	*Two survivors*
1928	RYE HARBOUR	*Seventeen*	*No survivors*
1939	ST IVES	*Seven*	*One survivor*
1947	THE MUMBLES	*Eight*	*No survivors*
1953	FRASERBURGH	*Six*	*One survivor*
1953	ARBROATH	*Six*	*One survivor*
1959	BROUGHTY FERRY	*Eight*	*No survivors*
1962	SEAHAM	*Five*	*No survivors*
1969	LONGHOPE	*Eight*	*No survivors*
1970	FRASERBURGH	*Five*	*One survivor*
1981	PENLEE	*Eight*	*No survivors*

At lunchtime on 13 December southerly winds of storm force, gusting to hurricane 12 were being recorded. Soon afterwards St Peter Port Signal Station picked up a message from the Danish ship *Charlottenburg*. The message was relaying a Mayday from an Ecuadorian merchant vessel, *Bonita*, listing 40° to starboard. There were 36 people on board including women and children.

Even before that St Peter Port lifeboat crew had assembled aboard their 52ft 'Arun' class lifeboat, *Sir William Arnold*, a vessel had broken adrift in the harbour and was in danger of fouling the lifeboat. Having heard from the Honorary Secretary that they may be needed to launch to the *Bonita*, the crew carefully checked their lifeboat for a prolonged service in heavy weather.

Soon the message came for them to launch. Torbay lifeboat on the other side of the Channel which might have been closer to the casualty was already occupied going to the help of a yacht. It was 14.00hr when the lifeboat headed out of harbour at full speed. The conditions she met were appalling: snow driven by the hurricane-force wind and sea spray reduced visibility

to 200yd. The sea was extremely rough and confused. Coxswain Michael Scales kept the lifeboat on a northerly heading at full speed; running before the southerly storm and sea there was always a risk of broaching and, sure enough, not long after setting out the lifeboat's stern veered round, presenting her beam to sea and wind. The Coxswain recovered his course and resumed full speed. Three-quarters-of-an-hour later, approaching the traffic separation zone in the Channel, the lifeboat broached again. In fact, she was to broach six more times on her way to the casualty, but throughout the Coxswain maintained full 18kt speed.

At 16.30hr, thanks largely to skilful use of Decca Navigator and radar in the very limited visibility, St Peter Port lifeboat arrived on scene. What happened next is graphically described in the account which appeared in the RNLI's journal *The Lifeboat*.

'The wind, from south-southeast, was still blowing at force 11 and this violent storm had created a sea of 15 metres. Visibility had improved and Coxswain Scales was able to see two helicopters and also four large vessels round the casualty, all well lit by deck lights. He knew that four people had been lifted off by a Sea King helicopter from RNAS Culdrose in daylight and flown to RNAS Portland, but all subsequent attempts at rescue had failed.

'*Bonita* was lying on a heading of 250°T, listing 45° to starboard, presenting her high side to the wind and rolling heavily. Her lee rails and stanchions were well in the water, as was the starboard wing of her bridge, and some seas were sweeping right over her decks. Several mooring ropes, drums and large pieces of timber were floating, trapped on her lee side.

'St Peter Port lifeboat approached the starboard midship area of the casualty and saw a man at the wheelhouse window. She then manoeuvred around the stern and found the crew of *Bonita* assembled on the high side of the ship, beneath the bridge. A pilot ladder was rigged near the crew. Coxswain Scales recognised that he could not effect a rescue from either side of the vessel and so indicated to the crew that they must make their way to the stern.

'One man attempted to move aft inboard of the rails. He fell, breaking his leg. His companions could do no more than lash him to the hatch to prevent his being swept overboard. The remainder moved aft clambering along the outboard, high side of the rails.

'At the stern Coxswain Scales found that his lifeboat was rising level with *Bonita's* after deck on each crest and falling below the bottom edge of her rudder in the troughs, a distance of 50 feet. He could not lie alongside the transom because the rudder projected beyond it and so he ran in, presenting his port side to the transom. Three men jumped to the lifeboat but their timing was poor and they fell some 25 feet to the deck. One man struck the lifeboat's stanchions and deckhouse and was badly injured. The lifeboat was swept round the stern into the debris, but, by using his outboard, starboard, engine only, Coxswain Scales was able to come clear without fouling his propellers and lie off down wind of the casualty.

'Coxswain Scales now approached head-on to the transom. Second Coxswain Peter Bougourd was stationed forward and the crew were stationed down the port side, all secured by their lifelines. While the lifeboat was held under helm and engines, some four to six feet from the transom, Second Coxswain Bougourd threw the heaving line aboard *Bonita*; the

Above:
The tragic moment when Fraserburgh lifeboat was capsized by a huge breaking wave. The outline of her bow can just be seen in the background. She had put out to a Danish fishing fleet reported in distress on 21 January 1970; five of her crew of six were lost.

wind prevented the line being passed from a greater distance. The run of the swell was trying to carry the stern of the lifeboat round the stern of the ship into the debris and the surge was trying to sweep her on to the deck of the casualty. Two women attached the heaving line around themselves. As they jumped into the sea, the lifeboat came gently astern on her engines until she was two boat lengths from *Bonita*. The survivors were then pulled to the lifeboat and recovered from the lower side deck aft. They were taken to the deckhouse where Motor Mechanic Robert Vowles attended to them. From a distance of five boat lengths the next approach was made.

'Five people were rescued in this way. Twice survivors let go of the line when they were in the water and then swam clear of the casualty. The lifeboat crew picked them up from the water when they came clear of the debris.

'At this time, about 17.15, the wind shifted to the north west and increased slightly. This further confused the sea to the stern of the casualty. One man, without a lifejacket, fell from the stern of *Bonita* while the lifeboat was recovering the next survivor. He was swept into the debris and down the starboard side of the motor vessel. Having recovered the survivor in hand, the lifeboat made off to search for the man who had fallen but *Charlottenburg* reported that she could see him and he appeared to be dead. Coxswain Scales returned to the casualty to take off more survivors.

'In the confused sea at the stern of the casualty the lifeboat continued to rescue survivors using the heaving line method. It was now imperative that the lifeboat was held with her bow at right angles to the centre of the transom, otherwise the wind or swell would have carried her round on to *Bonita's* quarters. Some runs in had to be abandoned in order to avoid severe damage to the lifeboat and during one violent astern manoeuvre first one engine, then the other, failed. Although both were restarted quickly, the bow of the lifeboat was trapped under the chine of *Bonita's* transom until the lifeboat's engines pulled her astern. Second Coxswain Bougourd remained in his very dangerous position forward.

'From an estimated total of 50 runs in to the transom, ten runs had to be made to take off one man. He sat without a lifejacket and with his legs over the side. Each time he caught the heaving line, but could not hold on to it. The Second Coxswain finally persuaded him to wrap the line around his hands and then pulled him into the sea.

'Having recovered 16 survivors Coxswain Scales took his lifeboat upwind of *Bonita* while he gave his crew a respite for a few minutes, in good view of the casualty. In the freezing temperature and constant heavy spray, circulation was restored, aching muscles were eased and lifelines were adjusted. Then the lifeboat once again approached *Bonita's* transom. During the respite, a helicopter made several attempted rescues and succeeded in lifting off one man.

'Using the heaving line method, the lifeboat crew continued to recover survivors, although frequently engulfed by seas coming aboard. One man was not breathing when he was lifted on board. Crew Member John Webster took instant action to expel water from his mouth before passing him into the wheelhouse. In the wheelhouse Motor Mechanic Vowles was helping the survivors out of wet clothes and then helping them down into the forward and after cabins, where the heaters were full on.

'The captain of *Bonita* was the last man to be recovered by the lifeboat. He confirmed that only one man remained on board. As he had a broken leg, he could not be moved to the transom. Royal Fleet Auxiliary *Olna*, which had accepted the duties of on-scene commander on her arrival at 17.06, told Coxswain Scales that a helicopter was returning, having refuelled, and would try to lift off the one remaining man. Coxswain Scales asked Brixham Coastguard that Torbay lifeboat, already nearing the scene, should continue coming to give the helicopter help. In view of the serious condition of his severely injured survivor, Coxswain Scales then set course for Brixham.'

The one injured man left aboard *Bonita*, strapped to the hatch cover, had a remarkable escape. Torbay lifeboat had steamed to within a mile of the stricken ship when she heard that he had been rescued by the French tug *Abeille Languedoc* which had been standing-by. Just over 15min after the departure of the St Peter Port lifeboat he was seen to slip from the

Above:
The crew of the lifeboat to make history in 1914. Tynemouth lifeboat, *Henry Vernon*, one of the RNLI's early motorised lifeboats, successfully rescued 50 people from the hospital ship *Rohilla* and in so doing proved the value of engines in lifeboats as opposed to oar power.
Courtesy of H. A. Straker

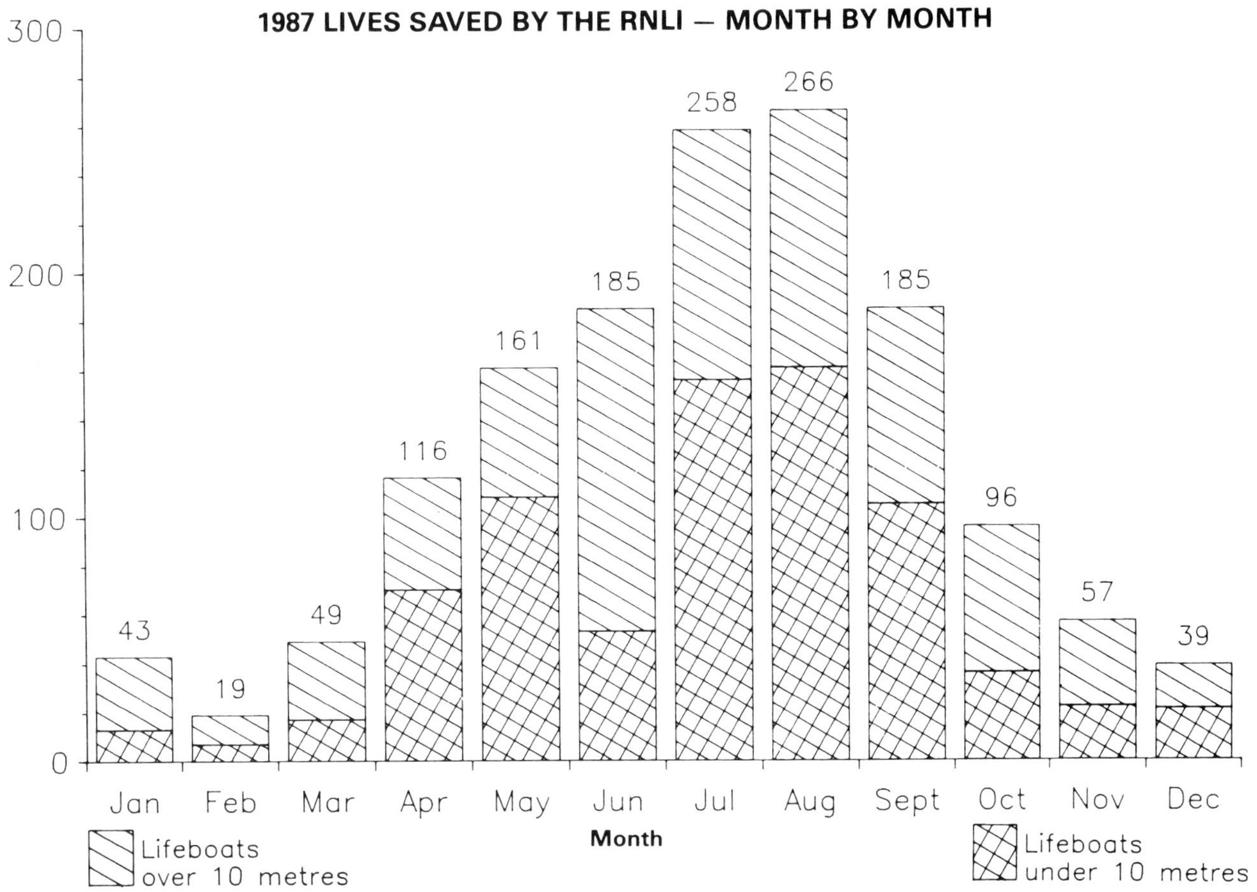
1987 LIVES SAVED BY THE RNLI — MONTH BY MONTH
300
200
100
0
43
19
49
116
161
185
258
266
185
96
57
39
Jan Feb Mar Apr May Jun Jul Aug Sept Oct Nov Dec
Month
Lifeboats over 10 metres
Lifeboats under 10 metres

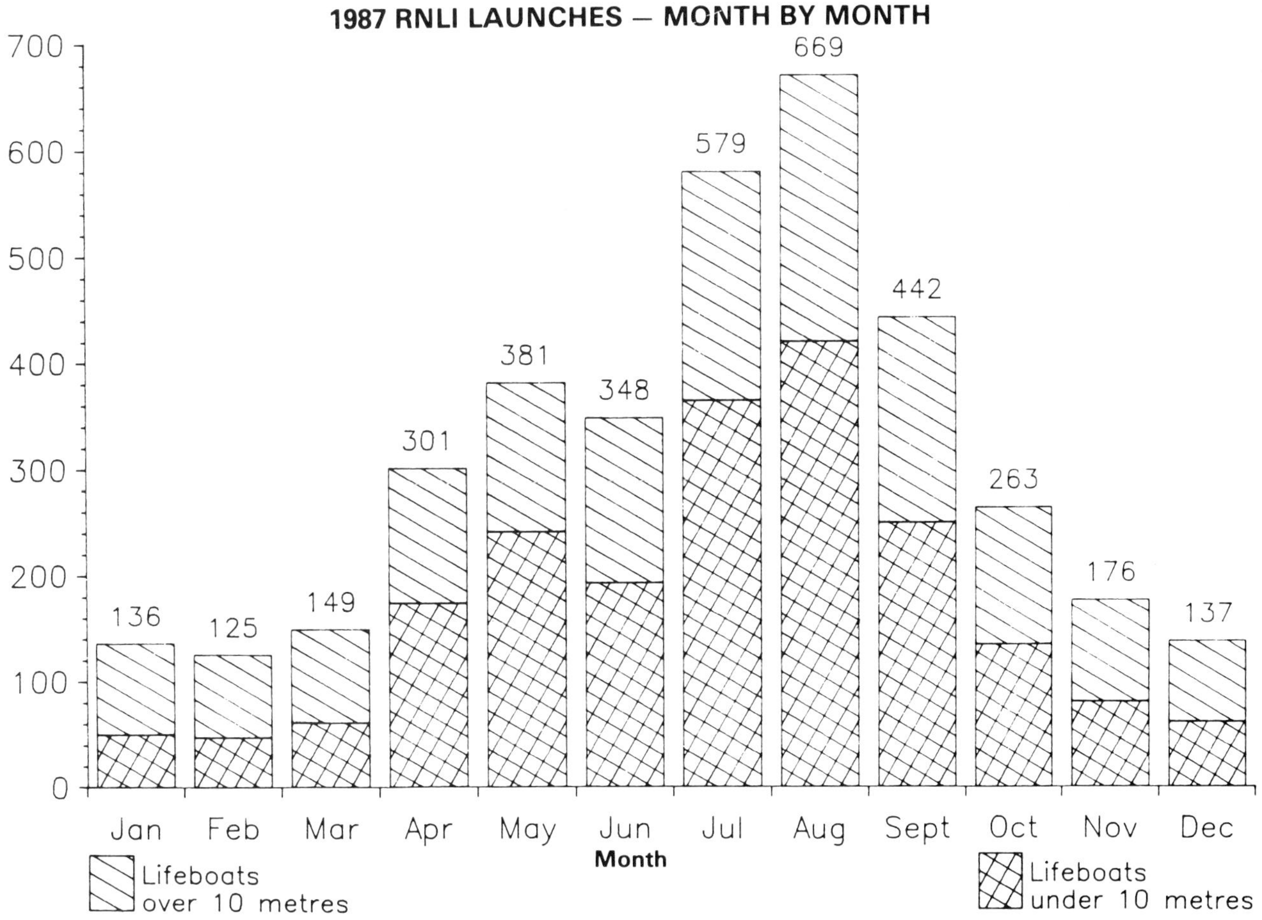
1987 RNLI LAUNCHES — MONTH BY MONTH
700
600
500
400
300
200
100
0
136
125
149
301
381
348
579
669
442
263
176
137
Jan Feb Mar Apr May Jun Jul Aug Sept Oct Nov Dec
Month
Lifeboats over 10 metres
Lifeboats under 10 metres

stern hatch cover, regain a handhold and finally fall into the sea. The tug's Captain waited till he was clear of the casualty's masts and then moved in and pulled him from the water.

Bonita was last seen at 05.00hr the next morning and was later confirmed to have sunk.

Right and below:
The RNLI awards Gold, Silver and Bronze Medals for gallantry to its lifeboat crews. There is also the Thanks of the Institution inscribed on vellum for services not quite worthy of a Bronze Medal. The obverse of the medal shows the head of the RNLI's founder, Sir William Hillary, and the reverse bears the inscription 'Let not the deep swallow me up'. *David Trotter*

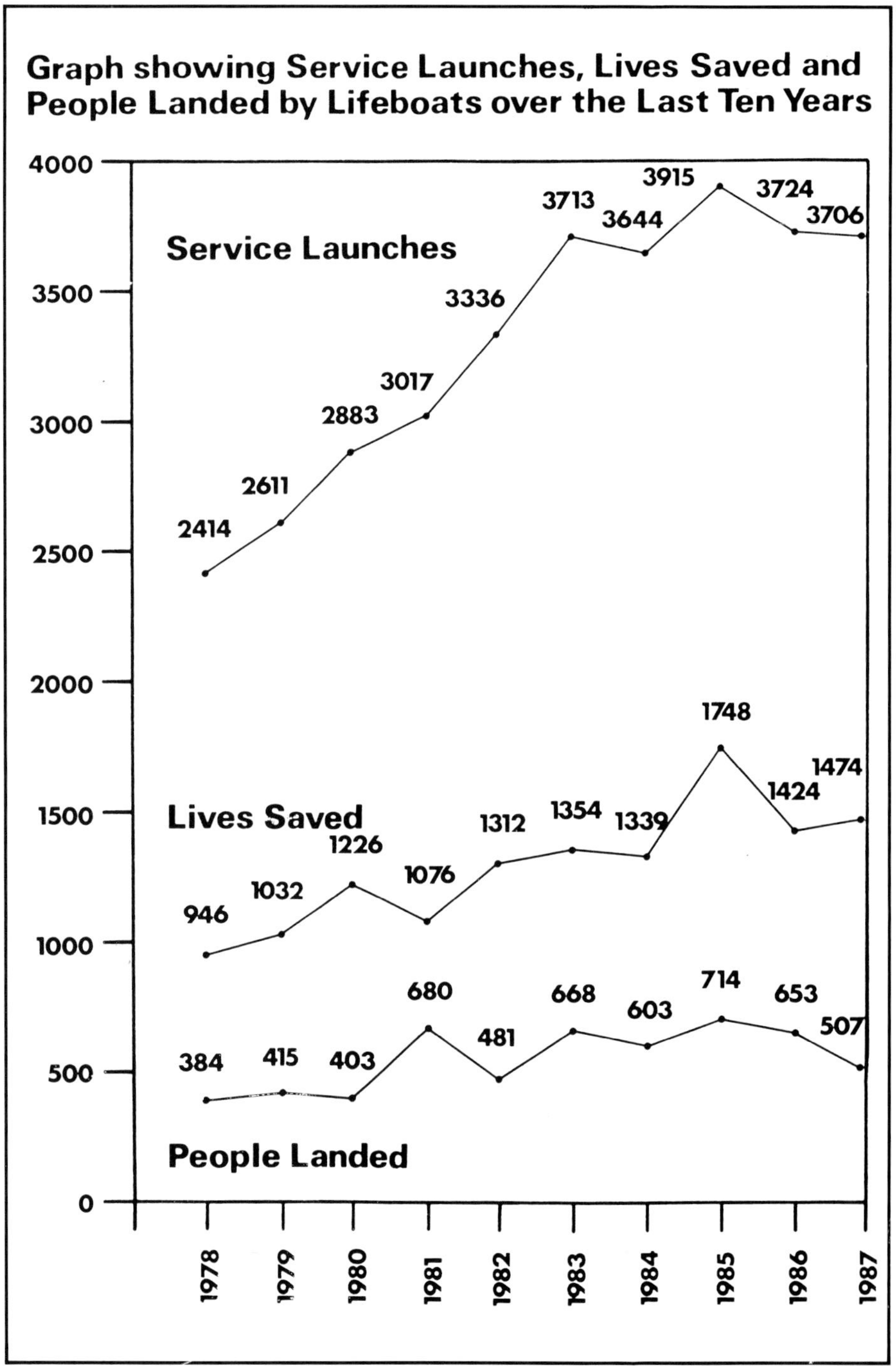

Other Medal Services

The last crewmember of a lifeboat under 10m to be awarded the Silver Medal was Arthur Hill (right), from Largs, Scotland. On 24 July 1983 he saved a girl who was trapped under the hull of an upturned motor cruiser. He jumped overboard from the Largs 'Atlantic 21' rigid inflatable lifeboat and dived underneath the upturned boat. With little air left and amid diesel fumes he succeeded in pushing the terrified girl down under the side of the boat so that she could be pulled to safety by the lifeboat's helmsman. He managed then to get himself out from under the boat unaided but was close to unconsciousness through lack of oxygen when hauled aboard the lifeboat.

Seven Dover men (below) launched into the notorious hurricane which hit the southeast of England on 16 October 1987. Acting Coxswain Roy Couzens was awarded the Silver Medal and each of his crew the Bronze Medal after they rescued three survivors from the sinking cargo vessel *Sumnia*.

Dover's 50ft 'Thames' class lifeboat launched into 20ft waves and winds registering force 16-17 to aid the stricken vessel which had been driven against the Admiralty Pier and was pinned against the western end of the southern breakwater. Acting Coxswain Couzens took the lifeboat very close to the breakwater to rescue two men who had been washed overboard. The vessel began to sink and the lifeboat searched for the other four crew members with huge seas engulfing her. At one stage the lifeboat fell off a 60ft wave and the Acting Coxswain was thrown heavily against the controls. A further survivor was rescued from the water and resuscitated.

RNLI Gallantry Awards

RNLI medals for gallantry can be Gold — for truly outstanding acts of bravery and seamanship — and Silver or Bronze. From 1824, in the reign of George IV, the medals carried the sovereign's head as Patron of the RNLI, but when George VI became King he ruled that the monarch's head should only appear on medals given by the monarchy. The portrait by A. G. Wyon of Sir William Hillary, the RNLI's founder, was introduced in 1938. The reverse stayed the same (three small figures hauling a drowning man into a small boat with the inscription 'Let Not The Deep Swallow Me Up', designed by William Wyon). Each medal is suspended by a blue silk cord ribbon from a bar formed by two dolphins. Gold Medals are very rare indeed and are sometimes referred to as the 'lifeboatman's Victoria Cross'. It was first awarded in March 1824, the same month that the RNLI was founded. Little is recorded of the rescue except that Cdr (later Adm Sir) Charles Freemantle, when on coastguard duties, had swum with a line to a Swedish brig wrecked off Christchurch, Hants. Since the RNLI was founded in 1824 the following medals have been awarded: Gold — 141; Silver — 1,543; Bronze (introduced 1917) — 721. The crew involved in a service resulting in the award of a medal are each presented with a medal service certificate.

The fourth award for gallantry is the Thanks of the Institution inscribed on vellum. This is a beautiful, illuminated certificate on parchment, signed by the President, HRH The Duke of Kent and the Chairman of the Institution.

The Aftermath of Three Silver Medal Services

Coxswain Ken Voice of Shoreham was awarded the Silver Medal after he brought his 42ft 'Watson' class lifeboat alongside the Greek cargo vessel *Athina B* four times to take off 26 people in a force 10 storm and violent seas in January 1980. The *Athina B* had broken down off Brighton beach where she finally grounded and was left high and dry as this picture shows (see also page 27). During the rescue the lifeboat was rising and falling 15ft in the surf alongside the casualty and, as the last man jumped for the lifeboat, he landed in the sea, and only the prompt action by coxswain and crew saved him from being crushed between the two vessels.

Hallur Helgeson, third engineer of the Icelandic coaster *Tungufoss*, received this welcome home from his son Halli at Reykjavik airport after his rescue from the seas off Cornwall by Sennen Cove lifeboat. On the night of 19 September 1981, Coxswain Maurice Hutchens earned the RNLI's Silver Medal in rescuing seven of the 11-man crew of the coaster in force 8 to 9 gales.

When the lifeboat reached the casualty she found that three of the 11 crew had been rescued by an RN helicopter, but the winchman had been injured. After two attempted approaches, the lifeboat was manoeuvred as close as possible to the casualty's stern and, one at a time, three men were transferred from the coaster to liferafts attached to her stern and floated towards the lifeboat where they were snatched aboard. Two more men tried to jump into the rafts which were filling with water but missed their footing and fell into the sea; they were spotted with the help of the helicopter's searchlight and pulled aboard the lifeboat. The coaster's list was increasing all the time, but with great skill the lifeboat was taken close in, avoiding the ship's rudder, so that two more men could leap aboard. With the coaster almost on her beam ends and apparently about to founder, the lifeboat began a final approach but the last man on board, the captain, managed to grab the lifting strop flown within his grasp by the helicopter and was lifted to safety.

All that remained of the fishing vessel *La Morlaye* on the morning after her crew of three were plucked to safety by Tynemouth lifeboat in a force 8 gale and 20ft rolling waves only a few hundred yards from the beach. Coxswain Captain John Hogg was awarded the RNLI's Silver Medal for this service. At first he tried to tow the fishing boat clear of the beach but when this failed he took the considerable risk of going alongside in the very shallow water while his crew pulled the survivors to safety.

The History and Structure of the RNLI

The RNLI Headquarters and Depot are a complex of offices, workshops, stores and services, each playing an essential role in providing the back-up for lifeboats and their vital work.

RNLI Headquarters

The Royal National Lifeboat Institution has its head office and main depot at Poole, Dorset. These were built in 1974/75. Before that time the RNLI was based in London but, by selling its buildings and moving to Poole, new freehold facilities were provided at no extra cost. For the first time in its long history, the administrative core of the lifeboat service is now situated in its own premises on the coast.

The Institution started life in the City of London, then the financial centre of the world; the first head office, occupied from 1824 to 1826, was at 12 Austin Friars. The office was moved to 18 Austin Friars in 1826 and remained there until 1836 when it was transferred to the first floor of number 20. In 1846, a further move was made to the second floor of 8 Great Winchester Street just around the corner from Austin Friars. The year 1851 was one of much reorganisation for the Institution, which had been without a President since 1828. The fourth Duke of Northumberland took on this office in 1851 and launched his famous competition for an efficient lifeboat design. Richard Lewis had recently been elected Secretary and it was shortly afterwards that reliable records began to be kept. Also, in 1851 the offices moved from the City to the Charing Cross district, where the headquarters stayed in different buildings for some 80 years. Premises were taken at 20 John Street, Adelphi, but after only three years the Committee of Management found 'more commodious premises' at 14 John Street almost opposite, and the move took place in 1855. It was to be the longest occupied head office in the RNLI's history and, although it was the expiry of the lease which caused the next change of premises, the building which was considered roomy in 1854 was hardly adequate 50 years later. The work of the Institution had more than doubled in this time and, once again, larger offices were needed. A 65-year lease was taken on 22 Charing Cross Road; the ground rent was £385 and the lease of £10,000 was considered moderate for such premises. It was felt that the offices were much better '. . . for the great national object of the Institution and far more sanitary and suitable for the officers and staff'. The Committee of Management was also well aware that such a prominent site would afford greater publicity to the RNLI. In

International Lifeboat Federation

In 1924, to mark the RNLI's 100th anniversary, the first International Lifeboat Conference was held in London. Seven other countries — Denmark, France, Japan, the Netherlands, Norway, Spain and the USA — were represented.

The exchange of ideas and knowledge was so welcome that International Lifeboat Conferences have been held every four years and the RNLI acts as secretariat. The name was changed to International Lifeboat Federation at the 16th conference held in Spain in 1987.

The lifeboat services of the world operate in widely differing circumstances — from the inland lakes of Switzerland to the frozen waters of the Arctic. Many of the societies are based on the RNLI, as it was the first lifeboat service in the Western world. Some remain voluntary such as Spain, Sweden, the Netherlands, New Zealand and South Africa, others are part government-run and part voluntarily funded, such as France and some, like the US Coastguard, are completely state-run.

Below:
New lifeboat designs begin in the drawing office.

1931, again because of lack of space and due to increasing work, the RNLI moved to 42-44 Grosvenor Gardens and this was to be its last move within London.

The move out of London came largely as a result of a report in 1971 by PA Management Consultants who were asked to review the organisation of the RNLI. The Committee of Management endorsed their recommendation that the head office and depot should be amalgamated and situated in the provinces. The site would need water frontage and would have to be within two hours' rail journey of London. In October 1972 two adjoining sites had been found in Poole and, in 1973, the gradual transfer of staff to temporary accommodation began. The transfer was effectively completed by February 1974 and on 30 October, the then Chairman of the Institution, Cdr F. R. H. Swann CBE, RN, laid the foundation stone of a new head office building. A stainless steel capsule containing historic documents, photographs and examples of the Institution's colours was placed under the stone.

CHRONOLOGY OF THE LIFEBOAT SERVICE

1771	Bamburgh Castle sea-rescue organisation in being
1786	Bamburgh administrators commission Lionel Lukin to convert a coble for rescue work
1790	Henry Greathead's *Original* lifeboat in service in South Shields
1823	Sir William Hillary's Appeal for a national sea-rescue service
1824	'National Institution for the Preservation of Life from Shipwreck' established
1851	Competition for designs of efficient lifeboats
1854	Change of name to 'Royal National Lifeboat Institution' Subsidy from the Board of Trade (relinquished 1869)
1890	First steam lifeboat in service
1897	Parliament fully satisfied with affairs of the RNLI following inquiry
1909	Motor lifeboats in service
1924	Centenary of the foundation of the RNLI First International Lifeboat Conference in London
1929	Introduction of radio telephony in lifeboats
1963	Introduction of inflatable lifeboats
1966	Introduction of the first Fast Afloat Lifeboat, the 'Waveney' class
1969	Introduction of the Yachtsmen's Lifeboat Supporters' Association (later Shoreline)
1971	Introduction of the 'Arun' class lifeboats
1972	Introduction of the 'Atlantic 21' rigid inflatable lifeboat
1982	'Arun' class first lifeboat to be awarded Design Council Award Introduction of the Fast Slipway Lifeboat, the 'Tyne' class
1988	Introduction of the Fast Carriage Lifeboat, the 'Mersey' class

RNLI Depot

For the first 60-odd years of the RNLI, all its lifeboats were fitted out at boatbuilders' yards with gear being ordered straight from the manufacturers. As the size of the fleet increased, it became necessary to establish the Institution's own storeyards with a storekeeper and riggers who would attend solely to RNLI work. The storeyard was opened at Poplar in 1882. Initially there were sheds for stowage of lifeboats and their carriages, an office for the storekeeper and two cottages for the chief and assistant riggers. The yard opened on to the bank of the Limehouse Cut canal, in which harbour trials (stability, self-righting etc) of new lifeboats were carried out before they were sent to their stations.

For more than 30 years there was little change to the storeyard, but with the development of motor lifeboats new equipment and a new shed were provided. After World War 1 the function was expanded when a machinery workshop was opened for minor repairs and for the manufacture of components which were difficult or expensive to obtain on the open market. As far as possible, a reserve lifeboat of each type was kept available for immediate despatch to the coast. The riggers were all ex-Naval men and various Naval traditions, including time keeping by bell, were used. In time, larger and more modern workshops were again needed and a new site was found at Borehamwood, Hertfordshire, which was chosen particularly for its excellent facilities for road transport, being on the A1 — the Great North Road.

The Depot was officially opened in July 1939 and within a few weeks the staff from the head office at Grosvenor Gardens moved in and stayed for the duration of World War 2. The move to the Borehamwood depot was timely, too, as London's dockland areas suffered severe bombing during the war years. The new depot was to provide stores for lifeboat stations and fund raising branches throughout the country. In addition to many thousands of items of lifeboat equipment — ranging from tiny screws to anchors and fuel tanks — a large publicity store was established to distribute collecting boxes, flags, decorations and souvenirs. A machine shop manufactured machinery parts, facilities existed for all kinds of repair work, tractors could be overhauled, and an examination department tested the incoming stores. Lifejackets were rigorously examined and the rigging loft — although less busy than in the heyday of pulling and sailing lifeboats — was still an essential part of the depot, providing ropes and ropework. There were carpenters, painters, a signwriter and an administrative staff. The Depot proudly boasted that it was constantly open for service, 24 hours a day, and could therefore despatch any item to a lifeboat station within an hour of being alerted.

The RNLI is managed by a Committee of Management who are all volunteers. It is composed of those who give the benefit of their knowledge in such fields as boat design and construction, medical matters, commercial, industrial, finance, investment and banking, public relations and other professions and skills. The Committee works through an Executive Committee and various sub-Committees, including Search and Rescue, Boat, Technical Consultative, Medical and Survival, Fund Raising, Public Relations, Establishment, Finance and Investment. The Director is responsible for the day-to-day running of the RNLI which employs a staff of over 600, 300 on the coast and in 14 regional offices throughout the country, and the rest in Poole. The Director reports to the Committees which meet regularly during the year.

With 204 lifeboat stations and an annual turnover of over £30 million, the lifeboat service needs an efficient Head Office and Depot. On the ground floor of the Head Office there is an entrance hall, a reception desk and sales kiosk. A small museum contains models, paintings and other interesting exhibits. On the other side of the entrance hall is the committee room. This is not only used for meetings but also for film and slide shows for visiting groups such as schools and other organisations. The first floor is occupied by the Accounts Department, the Data Processing Department and the Typing Pool. The Accounts Department handles the accounting functions of the Head Office, Depot, regional offices and nearly 2,000 branches and guilds nationwide. As well as the normal receipting and payments operations, a full system of budgetary control and statistical information is maintained through the computer. The Data Processing Department is responsible for operating the computers and has a development team maintaining, investigating, designing and installing systems and programs for the Institution's requirements.

The second floor houses the Technical Department and the Purchasing Department who work in close co-operation. The design and maintenance of lifeboats is undertaken by naval architects, engineers and surveyors supported by a drawing office of skilled draughtsmen. The Purchasing Department processes the purchase orders of all RNLI equipment and stores. Draughtsmen, surveyors, engineers and other technical experts design, test and

Below:
The Royal National Lifeboat Institution's head office moved to Poole from London in 1973/74.

Inset:
The workshop floor at the Poole Depot where skilled craftsmen make some of the equipment needed for the lifeboat fleet. The rigging loft can be seen on the right.

adapt lifeboats, their equipment and the tractors and carriages for launching. Lifeboats are designed in the RNLI's own drawing offices, sometimes from scratch and sometimes starting from a hull form which has been designed by an outside consultant.

The Fund Raising Department, which is located on the third floor, administers the RNLI membership scheme, payroll giving and many special appeals including those to charitable trusts, sporting clubs, shipping, industry and commercial promotions. A national lottery is also run with prize draws taking place each quarter. The RNLI receives large sums of money from wills, and the Legacies and Trusts Department handles millions of pounds every year.

The Public Relations Department is in frequent contact with the mass media and also has a small office in London. It organises films, posters, leaflets and publications on the RNLI including *The Lifeboat*. This magazine, containing news of all aspects of the service, has a circulation of over 100,000, about twice that of the largest yachting magazines. It is published quarterly, as is *Storm Force News*, the magazine for junior members. A Property Department deals with the legal and management aspects of boathouses, slipways and any other RNLI property or shore installation, including insurance, maintenance, repairs and new acquisitions. The Post Room, through which many hundreds of items pass daily, and the Central Filing System are also situated on the third floor.

At the top of the building are the offices of the Director and his Deputy. The Operations Division is another occupant of the fourth floor. A Central Operations and Information Room (COIR) is manned 24 hours a day every day of the year. Information of lifeboat services in difficult or complex situations are telexed through by the Coastguard. Movements of new and relief lifeboats are also organised from here, but the operations control of lifeboats remains with the local station Honorary Secretary and the Coxswain, who know local conditions and circumstances. They can ask for advice from COIR and may use the emergency facility to order replacements if equipment is damaged. The Operations Division has a rescue records section, which keeps details of all lifeboat rescues. These are fed into a computer which can produce analyses and maps to help with planning future lifeboat coverage, and find out more about the types of casualties and the reasons for call-outs. Lifeboat coverage is under constant review. As shipping and leisure boating patterns change, new stations may be opened and existing stations receive different types of lifeboat best suited to their area and casualties. The RNLI Communications Office looks after the communication and navigational aids such as radios, radar, direction finders, position fixing equipment and echo sounders. As this equipment becomes more complex, the crews need more training, so three caravans have been converted into mobile training units which tour the country providing training at the station. The Personnel Department is also housed on the fourth floor, and finally, the library with photographs of the RNLI's patrons and presidents, is used for meetings and houses historic lifeboat journals, records and reference books.

The Depot is alongside the RNLI Headquarters and has two sections to support the lifeboat fleet — the Stores and the Workshops. The Stores contain the range of spares that any lifeboat may need, from nuts and bolts to marine engines. Quality control is high and every incoming item is checked on entering the Stores. The complexity of the stock is due not only to the number of items that would be found on a new lifeboat, but also the fact that lifeboats have a life of 25 to 30 years, so some items which may be specific to one boat must be stored for a long time. It is impossible to standardise every item as availability changes and boats have different dimensions and power supplies. In some cases items are either so difficult or expensive to obtain commercially that they are made in the RNLI's own machine shop, where standards are extremely high. A rigging loft turns out work in both natural and synthetic material, with skilled riggers making bow puddings (rope bow fenders), scrambling nets, rope fenders, mats and various ropes and cables for launching and recovering lifeboats. The RNLI uses special lifejackets incorporating a light, whistle, strips of reflective material, a line for lashing to another survivor, a safety line, lifting strip and a mouth tube for inflation to give extra buoyancy; if inflated it automatically brings the wearer face-up in the water. The jackets are returned from the coast for periodic checks. Lifeboats also have regular surveys, with a partial check every year and a complete overhaul, often lasting several months, every five years. Equipment is updated and replaced at boatyards all around the coast, so stores must be sent out and items returned; this is undertaken by a small fleet of vans.

All support materials for the RNLI's branches and guilds are stored and despatched from the Fund Raising Support Centre on the Depot site. There are also regional depots in Hadleigh, Suffolk and Thirsk, Yorkshire. Collecting boxes, flags, posters, stickers, display materials, publicity caravans and boats are all handled here, while the printing section prepares special invitations, posters and leaflets for fund raising functions. An increasingly expanding and successful business for the RNLI is the sale of gifts and souvenirs. All RNLI items are carefully selected for quality and value and an illustrated brochure is available for mail order customers. Souvenirs and gifts are held here, and the mail order despatch for the whole country is carried out from this building.

The newest building on the site is a purpose-built self-contained Training Centre. All stations which are allocated new lifeboats send their crews to Poole where they undergo an intensive course in the new boat's equipment, capabilities and boat handling. This is followed by an extended passage to station, under the command of their Divisional Inspector and a further two weeks 'working up' period prior to the lifeboat's commencement of station duties.

Below:
The Central Operations and Information Room is manned 24hrs a day, all through the year.

The Greatest Lifeboatman

A CAREER SPANNING FIVE DECADES

'He was a big man in every sense of the word, a kindly genial man of exemplary character and possessing a youthful spirit; a magnificent seaman with the courage of a lion; a man of quick decisions and resolute action', said the Chief Inspector of Lifeboats in a tribute broadcast on radio in 1954 after the death of Henry Blogg of Cromer.

Henry Blogg was born in 1876 and joined the lifeboat crew in 1894 at the age of 18, in the era of pulling (rowing) lifeboats. He retired from the lifeboat service in 1948 at the age of 71 in the era of engine-driven lifeboats, after 38 years as Coxswain. The holder of three Gold and four Silver RNLI Medals for bravery, the George Cross and the BEM, Henry Blogg launched 387 times and helped save 873 lives, a record which earned him the title of 'The Greatest of all Lifeboatmen'.

When Henry was young few could have guessed how famous he would become for he was described as 'a spindle-shanked lad who never took part in games. He could not run and never learned to swim'. Brought up by his stepfather John James Davies he was already surrounded by lifeboats. His stepfather was Second Coxswain and *his* father, James Davies, was Coxswain; only the second coxswain there had been at Cromer. Henry was a good scholar: at the age of 11½ he was top boy in the top form, but was needed in his stepfather's crab boat. So Henry 'left Mr Hudson's school of reading, writing and arithmetic for his stepfather's school of baiting, hauling, rowing and seamanship' to become a longshore fisherman, catching cod from November to January and crab, herring and mackerel in the late summer and autumn; this left the summer free to help with the beach trade.

This was the era of the bathing machine. Henry Blogg directed the horses which drew the machines up and down the beach so that the Victorian ladies could step daintily straight into the water. The firm of J. J. Davies & Sons also ran a hire business, and Henry had a hut at the bottom of east gangway where, from a

Left:
A man of the sea, Henry Blogg was born in Cromer in 1876 and died there in 1954. No man has been more decorated as a lifeboatman. He won three Gold Medals, four Silver and was also awarded the British Empire Medal for his services.

large hamper, he supplied rough towels and bathing-dresses for a penny.

After six years of fishing with his stepfather Henry at last joined the lifeboat crew. He had wanted to join long before he was strong enough to take a man's place in the crew of the pulling boat, but he had to wait again for his first service — almost a year from January until 28 December 1894. The 17-man crew pulled to a dismasted ship in a hurricane and spent the night standing by until she could be guided towards safety. It was the custom to share out the rewards in the pub and on this first service Henry parted with some of his earnings, enough to cause him to vow next morning that he would never drink again and he did not.

In 1901 Henry married Ann Brakenbury, a Cromer girl; she was his strongest supporter, treasuring every reward and souvenir. On 26 September 1902 a son, Henry James, was born but died before he was two years old. On 5 December 1907 a daughter, Annie (called 'Queenie'), was born and was the apple of Henry's eye until her untimely death in 1935.

Henry loved children and his beach hut was often surrounded by prams. He was also a terrible tease and loved planning surprises but became desperately shy when the moment came to admit his part. He disliked conversation, particularly with officials and often avoided RNLI senior visitors, much to the embarrassment of the local Inspector of Lifeboats. However, he responded well to the holidaymakers and had a phenomenal memory for visitors' faces and names.

After only eight years in the lifeboat crew Henry became Second Coxswain, fast promotion for those days. His stepfather retired and James 'Buttons' Harrison took over as Cox. Only seven years later Henry was to become temporary Coxswain at the Annual General Meeting of the Cromer Branch on 13 January 1909: 'It was agreed that full authority be given to Henry Blogg to act as Coxswain during the temporary disablement of J. Harrison'. But by November it was clear that J. Harrison would never resume command, and a new Coxswain was needed.

Henry nearly did not make it, not because he was unsuitable, but because he was a teetotaller! The crew were afraid that he would stop their evenings in the bar, so when the votes were cast Henry narrowly squeaked home over George Rook — by one vote! In December, Henry's appointment was put to the committee and unanimously agreed by 60 fishermen. His first official duty as Cox (although he had been acting temporarily in this capacity for 10 months) was on 23 November 1909. The lifeboat saved 15 men from the 1,066-ton ship *Alf* during 15 hours at sea.

Henry was already making his mark outside Cromer and being noticed as one who hated fuss. Vice-Adm Sir John Cunningham once said: '. . . it was my duty a few weeks ago to read the minutes of an official inquiry into some work in which the Cromer lifeboat participated. If you read the evidence of Coxswain Blogg you would have thought that he had crossed the road to take the milk out of a baby's bottle'.

In 1917 Henry's fame was to spread far and wide with the award of his first Gold Medal for gallantry. The 38ft *Louisa Heartwell*, a pulling and sailing lifeboat was hauled across the sands and after an immense struggle was launched through the surf. Sixteen men were rescued from the Greek ship *Pyrin* after three hours hard rowing to reach her. The average age of the lifeboat crew exceeded 50 and some were nearly 70 years old (two-and-a-half years of war had taken away the young men). But that was not the end for another ship was in terrible trouble three or four miles out. The *Fernebo*, a Swedish ship, needed help but no other lifeboat could launch because the conditions were so terrible. Henry Blogg asked his crew the impossible but without any hesitation they

Above:
13 December 1933: the famous painting by Charles Dixon, RA, showing Cromer's No 2 lifeboat *Alexandra* driven by Henry Blogg on to the deck of the barge *Sepoy* so that her crew could be taken off.

Right:
Henry Blogg (far left), his dog Monty and his crew who helped him carry out the *Sepoy* rescue, photographed in front of their lifeboat soon after the event.

donned wet oilskins, lifebelts and sou'westers and started all over again. The *Fernebo* had been torn in half by an explosion and the two parts were gradually being driven on to the shore. The Cromer lifeboat made a valiant effort to launch but to no avail. Six men from the crippled ship took to a small boat which capsized as they neared the beach. A human chain hauled them, one by one, to safety.

Some hours later, in total darkness, another attempt was made to launch the lifeboat. The boat, brilliantly illuminated by searchlights set up on the cliff to shine on half the wreck at the foot, struggled again and again to clear the surf but a huge sea hit the *Louisa Heartwell* and broke five oars. A while later the tide had reached the point where the seaward flow from the breakwater was nearing the wreck. Henry called for his crew and gallantly they pulled out again using the flow to help them. At last the wreck was reached and 11 men were brought ashore — 14hr after the lifeboatmen first set out to the aid of the *Pyrin*.

In a letter to the editor of *The Lifeboat* Cdr Hall, wrote: 'It was his own remarkable personality and really great qualities of leadership which magnetised tired and somewhat dispirited men into launching, and when the boat was launched, it was the consummate skill with which he managed her and the encouragement he gave his crew which brought their efforts to such a successful conclusion.'

Henry was awarded the Gold Medal, the Second Coxswain the Silver, and 12 members of the crew the Bronze. The station that had not won an Institution medal in 60 years had won 14 in a single day.

The names of Henry Blogg and Cromer became synonymous with bravery and 10 years later a second Gold Medal was won when the lifeboat took off 15 men from another ship broken in two. The SS *Georgia*, a Dutch oil tanker, went aground on Sunday 20 November 1927 and broke her back. One half was swept away and SS *Trent* rescued 16 men from the hulk. But 15 men were stranded on the other part which was stuck fast on Happisburgh Sands. Great Yarmouth and Gorleston lifeboat could not get near so Cromer lifeboat was called upon to help. Blogg and his men had already been at sea for over a day guarding the abandoned half, not knowing the whereabouts of the crew. On seeing the wreck with waves tearing over her, Henry drove his *H. F. Bailey* motor lifeboat hard alongside using the tons of spilled oil from the wreck as a lee. Holed and waterlogged they landed the survivors after 28 hours at sea.

At the Annual General Meeting of the RNLI on 28 March 1928, HRH the Prince of Wales, President of the RNLI, said:

'. . . there is one little habit which I feel that Coxswain Blogg should break himself of and I am sure if there are any shipowners or marine underwriters here they would like me to bring this to his notice. Apparently he seems to regard it as an indispensable condition of the highest exercise of his seamanship, at any rate in Gold Medal cases, that the vessel must break in two. In the case of the *Fernebo* in January 1917, that vessel broke in two, each part floating away and coming to rest a mile or so apart on the rocks of Cromer, where Blogg rescued the crew of 11 after three heroic attempts in the pulling boat. In the case of the *Georgia* I notice that the vessel took care to follow the same procedure and therefore received Blogg's immediate attention. I know he will always be ready to launch his boat to the assistance of any vessel in distress and I can only suggest to him that he should not be too particular as to the precise number of pieces into which the wreck divides itself.'

What the Prince of Wales said when he heard of Henry's third Gold Medal service is unknown, but this time Blogg and his famous crew went out to help save the crews of no less than six merchant ships which had driven aground in thick fog on 5 August 1941. Convoy FS559 had been torn asunder by Happisburgh Sands. Blogg drove *H. F. Bailey*, Cromer No 1 lifeboat,

Above:
Cromer lifeboat reaches the scene of the wrecked *Sepoy* . . .

Below right:
. . . and the lifeboat drives on to the deck of the barge.

right on to *Oxshott* to rescue the 16 crew, and then using a line he veered down to *Gallois* and rescued 31 more. Having transferred these 47 survivors on to a destroyer, Blogg drove his craft on to the *Deerwood* and plucked a further 19 to safety. *Paddy Hendly* nearly caused their downfall for the water was so shallow that the lifeboat touched bottom more than once, whilst taking off a further 22 men. What a rescue! *H. F. Bailey* and Blogg landed 88 men, Cromer No 2 lifeboat *Harriot Dixon* landed eight, and *Louise Stephens* Great Yarmouth and Gorleston lifeboat landed 23 — a total of 119 men saved.

Henry Blogg, lover of good furniture, French clocks, good oil paintings and wall-plates retired as Coxswain in 1947 at the age of 70. Three years later his beloved wife Ann died and left her hero alone and lonely. On 4 January 1948 Henry carried out his last service, as number 7 in the crew, with Henry Davies his nephew as Coxswain.

On 19 August 1948 a new lifeboat was named at Cromer by Admiral of the Fleet Sir John Cunningham. Its name, *Henry Blogg*. An illuminated address presented to Henry on his retirement read: 'In the 72 years that you have lived in Cromer, and particularly during the 53 that you have served the RNLI, you have, by your deeds and example, brought great credit upon the town, which is proud to call you citizen, and upon the lifeboat service.'

Henry Blogg died on Sunday 13 June 1954. It was a mark of his renown that 2,500 people attended his funeral. A lorry carried 100 wreaths and the Coxswains of Sheringham, Wells, Caister and Gorleston shouldered the coffin. An ordinary man made great by his exceptional courage and service had passed on but his name is remembered by people worldwide. Henry Blogg of Cromer.

Right:
Coxswain Richard Evans, another legendary lifeboatman who won two Gold Medals in his time as Coxswain of Moelfre lifeboat. He is seen here with some of the grateful survivors from the Greek ship *Nafsiporos* whose rescue in December 1966 won Coxswain Evans the second of his Gold Medals.

Later Heroes

Coxswain Richard Evans, BEM

Moelfre Lifeboat 1921-70

Richard Evans is the only lifeboatman alive to hold two RNLI Gold Medals

Joined Moelfre, Anglesey, lifeboat crew 1921, aged 16. Bowman 1930-39; Second Coxswain 1939-54; Coxswain April 1954-January 1970; 49 years' service; launched 179 times; saved 281 lives.

First Gold Medal 27 October 1959
Rescued eight men from the motor vessel *Hindlea* in hurricane force winds gusting to 104mph. Lifeboat went in 10 times and once almost capsized by a huge breaking sea.

Second Gold Medal December 1966
Rescued 10 men from Greek motor vessel *Nafsiporos* in winds of over 127mph. Coxswain Evans, then over 60, was at the wheel for more than 12 hours.

Also awarded the Thanks of the RNLI inscribed on vellum in 1940, an RNLI Bronze Medal in 1943, the Queen's Silver Medal for Gallantry in saving life in 1960 and three war service medals for his time in the Merchant Navy.

'Man of the Year' in 1967; BEM 1969; 1970 subject of the TV programme 'This is Your Life'. 1975 made an honorary fellow of Manchester Polytechnic and in 1978 an Honorary Bard at the National Eisteddfod, being admitted to the highest order of the Druids.

Superintendent Coxswain Brian Bevan

The only serving lifeboatman to hold four medals for gallantry. Became only lifeboatman to receive three medals at one presentation and is the only serving lifeboatman to hold the Gold Medal

Professional seaman; joined Bridlington, Yorkshire lifeboat crew January 1967; appointed Superintendent Coxswain of Humber lifeboat station in 1975 at the age of 28 (the only lifeboat station manned by a full time crew).

Silver Medal 30 December 1978
Rescued six people including a woman and a girl from a Dutch coaster in very heavy seas, gales, blizzards and sub-zero temperatures.

Gold Medal 13 February 1979
In heavy seas, gales and snow showers the lifeboat was driven into the stricken coaster *Revi* which was rising 20ft above the lifeboat's deck. Over 30 approaches were made to take off the crew of four and the captain minutes before the ship sank.

Bronze Medal 15 February 1979
Launched to escort a listing cargo vessel through 40ft waves to the safety of the Humber Estuary. The service lasted 14hr.

Bronze Medal 13 December 1981
Rescued three people from a listing coaster in heavy seas, blizzards and force 10 gales, going alongside the ship eight times.

1980 — Subject of TV programme 'This is Your Life'.

Left:
Coxswain Brian Bevan of Humber lifeboat. He made history in May 1979 when he was presented with three medals for gallantry, a Bronze, a Silver and a Gold, all earned within a year. No other lifeboatman has been so honoured. He was awarded a futher Bronze Medal in 1981.
Margaret Murray

Below:
Coxswain Ken Voice of Shoreham was awarded a Silver Medal for his part in the rescue of 26 people from the Greek cargo vessel *Athina B* in January 1980. The vessel is seen here high and dry on Brighton beach where she finally grounded. (See also p18.)

So you want to be a Lifeboatman?

Left:
A mobile training unit outside the RNLI's permanent training centre at Poole. The mobile units tour the country's lifeboat stations giving lessons to crew members in radio operation and procedures, the use of radar and other electronic equipment.

Below:
The Neil Robertson stretcher is carried aboard all lifeboats over 10m. How to use it is part of the first aid training all lifeboat crews receive. *David Trotter*

Left:
This is a moment of real emergency during an exercise organised in 1986 to test lifeboats' ability to take off survivors from a stricken Channel ferry. A liferaft crowded with 'survivors' began rapidly to deflate and Ramsgate's 44ft 'Waveney' class lifeboat had to come in quickly alongside to take the occupants aboard.
Jim Byrne

A lifeboatman in the 1800s was probably a fisherman, wise in the ways of the sea and knowing his coast as well as his village streets. The main skill required was an ability to pull an oar and the determination to reach the wreck, however hard the task. What does it take to be a lifeboatman today?

One hundred years on, two major changes have taken place. The lifeboatman is far less likely to be a fisherman: his job could be anything from garage mechanic to teacher to company director, and the skills required of him are to be able to operate some of the most sophisticated equipment in the maritime world.

The RNLI has always trained its crews. Even in the days of oars and sails, top-hatted Lifeboat Inspectors made regular visits to stations. However, the accent on training has increased during the last 15 years, culminating in a rigorous series of courses both on station and at RNLI Headquarters.

Firstly, the 204 lifeboat stations are split into seven divisions, each with its own Lifeboat Inspector. The Inspectors are Master Mariners from the Merchant Navy or ex-Royal Navy seaman officers. Every six months the Divisional Inspector carries out a full inspection of each station, taking the lifeboat to sea. The drills may include such items as man overboard, blind pilotage, rigging the breeches buoy, setting the emergency steering, and working with a helicopter.

Between the Inspector's visits the Coxswain will hold regular exercises afloat. This gives the chance for more training, particularly of new crew members. The RNLI's 'Green Book' of regulations requires that each lifeboat exercises once every four weeks. At least one exercise per year must be carried out at low water. Rough water practice is essential including, for most classes, exercising in darkness.

These exercises are the breeding ground for new lifeboatmen and women. Anyone over 17 can join a lifeboat crew as long as they have a good knowledge of the local coastline and sea conditions, experience in boat handling, can pass the RNLI's medical examination and, most important of all, are acceptable to the rest of the crew, and approved by the Coxswain and the Divisional Inspector. Once accepted, the lifeboatman works his way up from helping to launch the lifeboat to playing a full part as a crew member. Apart from the exercises, crews are trained on station in two ways.

The first is by using the specially produced training videos and handbooks in the comfort of his own home. Subjects covered include chartwork and basic navigation, radio communication, liferafts, and specialised handling techniques for lifeboats of the 'inshore' type.

The second is by attending a course in one of the RNLI's Mobile Training Units (MTUs) at his station. The three MTUs — two for radio communications and navigation, and one for radar, are specially equipped caravans towed by a Land Rover. They visit lifeboat stations on a rotational basis during the evenings, and the Staff Instructor responsible for each MTU trains the crews to a standard which enables them to be examined for the appropriate certificate.

In addition, at least four members of each crew must be proficient in first aid. The Honorary Medical Adviser at each station certifies that the men have produced a recognised certificate in first aid from an approved organisation, such as the St John Ambulance Brigade. A course specifically designed for the needs of the lifeboat first aider is being constructed to train 'in house' in the near future. Equally important, three members of the crew must be proficient in handling the boat's engines. Each station has a full-time mechanic and he must train his own assistant and the emergency mechanics: their proficiency is then certified by the District Engineer. Some crews also have Lifeboat Signalmen, able to signal by light and to send and receive Morse code. Each proficiency rating is rewarded by the payment of a small proficiency fee.

Away from the lifeboat station the RNLI operates a variety of training courses. The most intensive is the sea training course at RNLI Headquarters, Poole, Dorset. This course is for the Coxswain and crew of a station which has been allocated a new class of lifeboat. Changing from a lifeboat built 20 years ago and capable of 8kt, to a totally modern craft capable of 18kt and full of complicated electronic aids can be quite a transition. It is therefore essential that the crew are familiar with the operation of the new lifeboat before having to use her in an actual rescue. To this end the crew spend five days carrying out a variety of practical exercises and lecture room sessions before sailing their new lifeboat on a prolonged passage to her station under the command of the Divisional Inspector and a District Engineer. As already explained, a further two weeks are spent 'working up' the whole crew before the new lifeboat takes over as the station lifeboat.

Similarly, special courses are run for the crews of 'Atlantic 21' rigid inflatable lifeboats. These are carried out at the RNLI's base in Cowes, Isle of Wight, where the boats are assembled. Crews at stations where an 'Atlantic' is to be placed for the first time join with crews on a 'refresher' course. The four-day course involves all aspects of boat handling and operation, mostly at sea. It also includes being capsized in the lifeboat and training to right her, re-board, re-start and continue operating. Two further courses have been introduced at RNLI Headquarters in Poole. The Honorary Secretary is in charge of the day-to-day running of the lifeboat station and has the authority to launch the lifeboat. From time to time a dozen or so of these men or their deputies — all volunteers — meet in Poole for a two-day course. Not only do they meet the Headquarters staff face to face, with whom they work so closely (so that they can be brought up to date on RNLI policy and future plans) but, almost more importantly, they get the chance to talk amongst themselves and to share similar problems and experiences. Courses for Coxswains and other boats' officers are now held at Poole; detailed advanced training using a radar simulator system, together with involved exercises at sea, test the man and improve his knowledge and ability especially when tasked with the duty of 'on the scene commander' where the Coxswain of a lifeboat may be co-ordinating the search at sea, of a number of other vessels. Once again, an opportunity to share ideas is one of the most beneficial aspects of the course.

Once a year the RNLI organises a major exercise, designed primarily to test the ability of lifeboatmen to deal with injured casualties — eg from fire, chemical leakage or explosion at sea. The 'Medex' involves two or three lifeboat stations, as well as the local Coastguard, the Maritime Rescue Co-ordination Centre, the local SAR helicopters, police and harbour authorities. The part of casualties is often played by servicemen realistically and horrifically 'made-up' and all is carried out under the keen eyes of the RNLI's senior operations staff and members of the RNLI's Medical and Survival Committee, again volunteers and experts in their own wide and varied fields.

In 1986 the RNLI was 'loaned' a passenger ferry by Sally Line and an evacuation of 98 Royal Marines and WRNS, acting as passengers, was carried out. This was the first time a 'Ferex' had been carried out at sea and illustrated the difficulties and successes of such an evacuation.

The RNLI may be manned by volunteers but they are as professional as their full-time counterparts in other countries. This was illustrated when two lifeboatmen went to America to carry out a course in rough weather handling on a similar class of lifeboat to their own. Although they were 'competing' against full-time US Coast Guards, it was one of the RNLI Coxswains, a volunteer, who won the award for the best boat handling. As the RNLI slogan reads: RNLI . . . Modern . . . Efficient . . . Voluntary.

Below:
It takes skill both for helicopter pilots (here of a Royal Navy Wessex HU5) and a lifeboat helmsman (here of an 'Atlantic 21') to transfer a casualty from boat to aircraft. Experience has shown that the manoeuvre is best performed while both are under way.

Below:
The ability to use a line gun accurately could mean life or death to a grounded casualty. *David Trotter*

Bottom:
To quell a fire may one day be the safest way of saving a life aboard a wreck. This exercise is taking place aboard a 47ft 'Tyne' class lifeboat. *Derek Berwin*

Modern Lifeboats

Right:
The 44ft 'Waveney' class lifeboat *The White Rose of Yorkshire* tackles heavy surf off Whitby. *Doran Bros*

Below:
Newhaven's 52ft 'Arun' class lifeboat *Keith Anderson* undergoing self-righting trials in 1985. The RNLI won a Design Council award for the design of the 'Arun'. There are currently 43 of the class in service.

Under 10m

As more people began using the sea for leisure purposes the number of inshore incidents increased. Conventional lifeboats with displacement hulls were unsuitable for dealing with capsized dinghies or bathers in difficulties. The need arose for simple inflatable high-speed rescue craft. The following is an outline of the types of boat in use ***under 10m.***

In June 1963 the RNLI brought into service, for the summer months only, light inflatable lifeboats of about 16ft (4.34m) in length. It was to be a landmark in the RNLI's history. Constructed of a tough nylon material, the boats needed just two crew, were capable of over 20kt and driven by a single 40hp outboard engine. Aberystwyth, Gorleston, Redcar, Wells, Mudeford, Southwold and West Mersea were the first stations to test the new breed of lifeboats introduced to cope with a growing number of casualties close to the shore.

As more people began using the sea for leisure purposes during the 'swinging sixties', the number of inshore incidents increased dramatically. Conventional 8kt lifeboats with displacement hulls were not designed to deal with capsized dinghies, air beds being blown out to sea or bathers cut off by the tide. A simple high-speed rescue craft was needed, and in 1962 the RNLI bought an inflatable lifeboat for extensive trials. It also sent a small delegation to France where the Breton Lifesaving Society were successfully operating similar boats and were most willing to offer help and advice. Their virtues were their speed of 20kt, an ability to go alongside other craft or persons in the water without causing or suffering damage, quickness of launching, ability to drive on to the beach at speed in an emergency and low running costs.

The performance of the eight inshore boats in that first year, launching 39 times and saving 10 lives, persuaded the RNLI to place a further 19 on service the next year. By 1966 the number of inflatable boats had risen to 72, with 32 remaining on station all through the year, a proof of their success. Today, there are 84 16ft (4.34m) 'D' class lifeboats on station with 27 operating all year. Although limited to operating in daylight and moderate weather conditions, the boats carry out over a third of all lifeboat work.

At its base at East Cowes, Isle of Wight, the RNLI soon began modifying and developing the inflatable lifeboats, inserting inner tubes to prevent air from leaking out. Floorboards able to take the strain of high speed were developed and foam rubber mattresses to help safeguard the crews from excessive injury were added.

Because of the pounding the boats gave their crews, an upper age limit of 45 was imposed and new young recruits were found. The volunteers needed a high degree of skill to handle the inflatables in choppy seas, surf and amongst rocks, and frequently showed courage and determination.

Until 1985 the lifeboats were purchased as bare hulls from either a French or UK manufacturer, and fitted out at Cowes base. However with experience gained over 20 years, RNLI staff have designed and developed the Institution's own 16ft inflatable, in conjunction with Avon inflatables. The RNLI/Avon lifeboat has improved seakeeping, stability, manoeuvrability and seakindliness, and gives a smoother ride to crews and survivors. With 20 already in service, these boats will continue to replace the older 'D' class

Below:
The 'Atlantic 21' is the RNLI's fastest lifeboat, capable of 30kt and with a 45-mile radius of action. Since the design was introduced in 1972, 'Atlantic 21s' have saved over 3,000 lives.

Above:
The first 'C' class twin-engined inflatable lifeboat was introduced in 1979. In the event of a capsize, the lifeboat can be righted manually using a method specially devised by the RNLI. She also has a buoyancy system which allows the lifeboat to continue on service even if her bow is punctured.

Below:
The three-man crew sit on a console inside the lifeboat, the helmsman steering with one hand on the wheel while adjusting the throttles with the other. The console unit contains radio, compass, controls, batteries and other equipment. Crews of 'Atlantic 21' lifeboats undergo special training at the RNLI's Cowes base.

Above:
The 52ft 'Arun' class lifeboat *Roy and Barbara Harding* stationed at Galway Bay on the west coast of Ireland. The RNLI runs all the lifeboat stations in both Northern Ireland and in the republic.

Left:
Girvan's 33ft 'Brede' class lifeboat *Philip Vaux* seen here off the Ayrshire coast.

lifeboats. Communication is by a commercial VHF radio modified by RNLI technical staff and fitted into an RNLI-designed fully waterproof container. Should the lifeboat capsize, a righting drill has been devised and the radio will still operate. Other equipment items include flexible fuel tanks, flares, anchor, first aid kit, compass and knife.

In the early days, crew members wore the same yellow oilskins and black rubber boots as the crews of conventional lifeboats. Now, one-piece rubber dry suits, boots and white helmets with visors provide the warmth, comfort and protection needed in the fast, open boats.

The success of the 'D' class inflatable lifeboat led to the development and introduction of other lifeboats under 10m in length. The RNLI experimented with several designs, including the Hatch boat, the Dell Quay Dory, the MacLachlan and the Boston Whaler. By the end of the 1960s it was obvious that a larger lifeboat, which could operate at night, was needed. After testing various rigid hull boats, the RNLI chose one pioneered by Rear-Adm

Above:
Since the 16ft 3in 'D' class lifeboat was introduced in 1963, it has become the busiest in the RNLI fleet. Yachtsmen, dinghy sailors, windsurfers and bathers cut off by the tide are all regularly rescued or helped by inflatable lifeboats.

Desmond Hoare at Atlantic College, South Wales. The boat had a rigid wooden hull topped by a sponson or tube. The shape of the hull allowed the boat to be pushed through the water by her twin outboard engines at greater speed than was possible in inflatables, and the sponson provided stability. Once again, RNLI engineers and technicians at Cowes base developed the design, incorporating strength, stability and the special equipment needed for lifeboat work.

In 1972 the first 'Atlantic 21' 'B' class lifeboat went into service at Hartlepool. Before long, in October that same year crew member Douglas Gibbin won a Bronze Medal for an outstanding rescue. A small sailing dinghy had capsized in severe weather and sea conditions. One of the two occupants, a 16-year-old boy, was thrown into the sea. Douglas jumped into the sea himself with a line and eventually managed to reach the boy, saving him from drowning.

Improvements and innovations to the 21ft (6.4m) 'Atlantic 21' have made her a sophisticated craft. The hulls, now made of glass reinforced plastic (GRP), are delivered bare to Cowes base where the sponson is secured to the hull and the lifeboat is fully fitted out by RNLI staff. A rollbar assembly above the engines on the stern of the boat provides the mounting for a righting bag, stowed flat. In the event of a capsize, a crew member from the water pulls a ring which activates a gas bottle and inflates the air bag. The lifeboat turns upright in a few seconds. The twin outboard 50hp engines, which give the boat a top speed of 30mph, are inversion proofed to enable them to restart after capsize, using a patented invention devised by the RNLI.

The three crew sit on the delta-shaped console in the centre of the lifeboat, the helmsman steering with one hand on the wheel while adjusting the throttles with the other hand. In this way, he can avoid difficult seas by going round them or outpacing them.

The 'Atlantic 21' has attracted world-wide attention. Several overseas lifeboat societies have bought them and sent crews to join with their RNLI counterparts for special training at Cowes base. Currently, there are 39 'Atlantic 21s' stationed in the UK and they have launched a total of over 9,000 times and saved over 3,000 lives.

The youngest member of the RNLI's under-10m lifeboat fleet is the 'C' class, developed from the Zodiak Mk IV, the first one being stationed at St Abbs, Berwickshire in 1979. The 17ft 6in (5.33m) inflatable lifeboat, powered by twin 40hp outboard engines, has a top speed of 27kt and can operate all the year round at locations where it is not possible to operate an 'Atlantic 21'. RNLI-designed equipment enables the lifeboat to be manually righted in the event of a capsize and she has a buoyancy system which allows her to continue on service even if the bow is punctured.

The relatively low cost of lifeboats under 10m, compared with the bigger lifeboats, has meant that they are an attractive target for funding by many firms, organisations and individuals.

The History of Cowes Base

The RNLI has used Cowes shipyards since 1913 when J. E. Saunder's yard was contracted to build a number of pulling and sailing lifeboats. Lifeboats over 10m are still built at Cowes by FBM Marine Ltd and Souter Shipyard Ltd. The Minerva yard, site of the present Cowes base, was first used by the RNLI in 1930 as stores and offices for overseers responsible for the lifeboats being built at the yards of J. S. White, Groves & Gutteridge and William Osborne at Littlehampton. The RNLI's timber stores, for building and repairing wooden lifeboats, used to be on site.

The RNLI first introduced 'D' class inflatable lifeboats into its fleet in June 1963, to cope with the growing number of people using the sea for leisure purposes and getting into difficulty close to the shore.

In 1967, the repair and maintenance work for inflatable lifeboats and outboard engines began at the yard and more buildings and land were acquired as the fleet of lifeboats under 10m increased.

Under the Superintendent (Cowes base) some 60 staff — supervisory and technical, fitters, boatbuilders and office staff — work together as a team giving support to the coast on all aspects of inflatable and rigid inflatable boat supply and maintenance.

Over 10m

The RNLI has committed itself to completing the introduction of fast lifeboats at every station by the year 1993. In so many of today's rescues the time taken to reach a casualty is crucial in deciding the success or failure of the mission. A rudderless yacht, a broken-down fishing boat, a capsized speedboat all need rapid reaction from the lifeboat service. Here are some of the fast, over-10m lifeboats the RNLI keeps on station to cope with every eventuality.

47ft (14.34m) 'Tyne' class

Introduced in 1982, this 18kt lifeboat was the first 'fast' lifeboat designed to launch down a slipway. There are 31 slipway lifeboat stations around the coast and by 1993 the RNLI plans to have 40 'Tyne' class in operation. This includes a number in the relief fleet, but so successful has the design proved that at some stations where the lifeboat can be kept afloat, a 'Tyne' class has been allocated.

She has a steel hull with a shallow draught, a long, straight keel and extended bilge keels together with partial tunnels to protect the propellers — all essential for slipway launching and working in shoal waters. A semi-planing hull which lifts the boat clear of the water's drag under power gives her an 18kt maximum speed. Self-righting is achieved by the watertight wheelhouse which, with its trapped air, will push the capsized lifeboat upright in 8sec.

The lifeboat is fitted with MF and VHF radios, radar, automatic direction finding units for both MF and VHF, echo sounders, an intercom system and a Decca Navigator. She carries first aid equipment, blankets, emergency rations and rescue gear and there is space for two stretchers. Survivors are placed in the forward and after cabins.

Steering is by twin rudders which have both power-assisted and hand-hydraulic controls. The diesel engines draw fuel from two main tanks, holding 510gal of diesel between them and there is a reserve tank holding 102gal. Trim planes are fitted to alter the running trim in varying sea conditions.

Length: 47ft (14.3m)
Beam: 15ft (4.6m)
Displacement: 24 tons (24.4 tonnes)
Draught: 4ft 2in (1.3m)
Engines: Twin 425hp General Motors 6V-92-TI diesels
Speed: 18kts
Radius of action: 120nm
Crew: 6

52ft (15.9m) 'Arun' class

The 'Arun' class was the first home-produced fast afloat lifeboat of the RNLI. Introduced in 1971 there are now 43 in service, the first three built with wooden hulls and the rest in glass reinforced plastic, except for a solitary steel-hulled boat stationed at Aith in the Shetlands. The 'Arun' has proved a highly successful design, winning a Design Council award in 1982 and proving herself time and again in the very worst of weather. Three of the four most recent Gold Medal rescues were carried out by this class of lifeboat.

Right:
The RNLI's newest design, the 12m 'Mersey' class, launches from her carriage at Hastings. A building programme has begun which will replace the 8kt wooden-hulled carriage-launched lifeboats around the coast with this 17½kt successor.

Below right:
An impression by the marine artist David Cobb of the 44ft 'Waveney' class lifeboat stationed at Troon when, in September 1980, her Coxswain Ian Johnson won the RNLI's Silver Medal for rescuing five men from a dredger in a gale and 20ft waves.

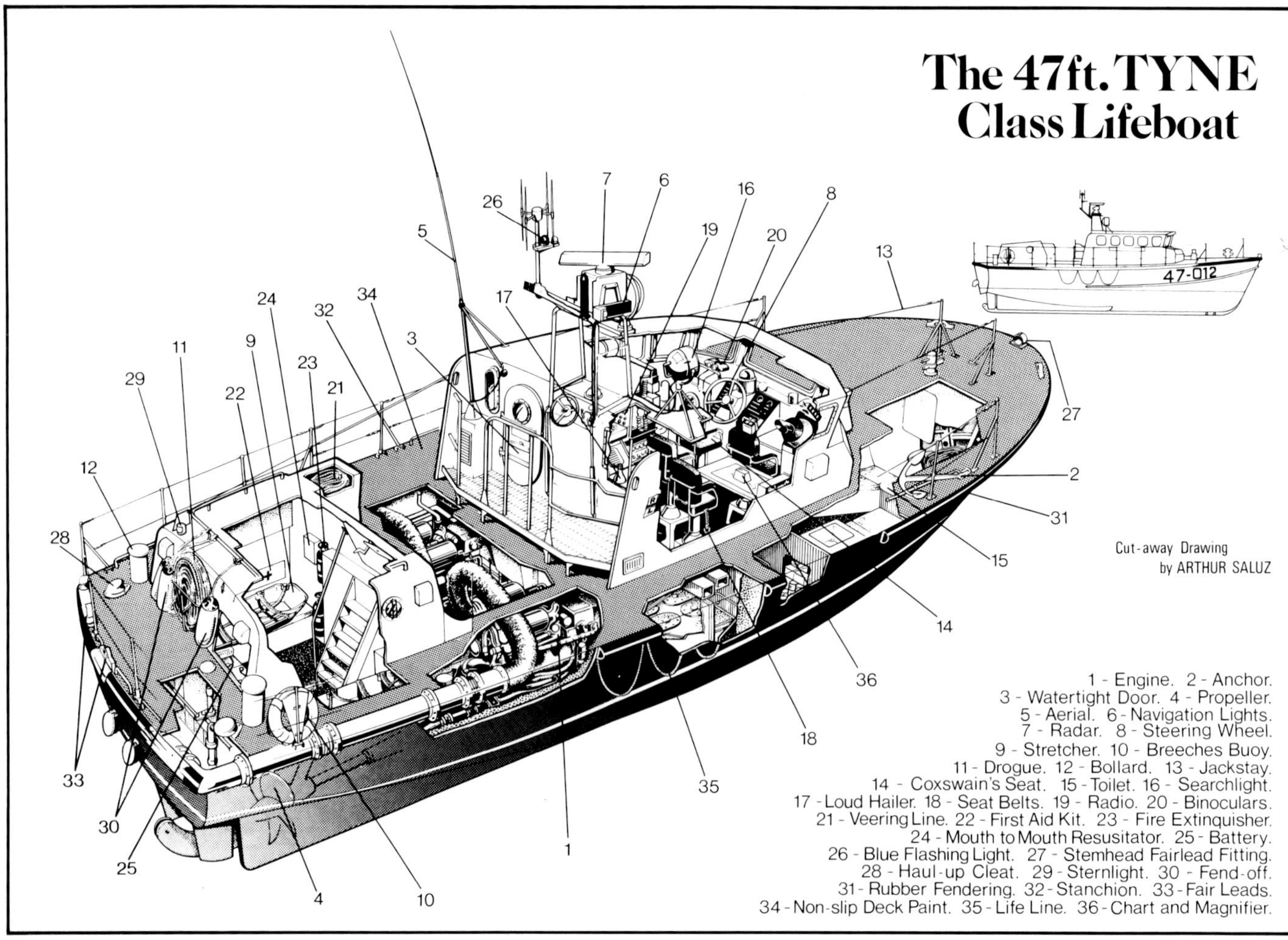

12-002

44-00

Above:
The prototype 12m 'Mersey' class lifeboat during her trials in heavy seas off Scarborough.
Scarborough and District Newspapers

She is self-righting thanks to her watertight wheelhouse; her hull is divided into 26 watertight compartments with void spaces filled with buoyant materials giving reserve buoyancy should she be holed. There are two cabins below deck for survivors containing rescue equipment including first aid gear, stretchers, emergency rations and blankets. An inflatable boat and liferaft are carried. The Coxswain can steer from inside the wheelhouse or from a flying bridge on top of the superstructure. Intercom links the flying bridge, wheelhouse and deck.

Inside the wheelhouse there is a seat with safety belts and armrests for each member of the crew. There are special positions for the Coxswain, navigator, radio operator, mechanic and crew members, and provision for a doctor.

A comprehensive range of communications and navigation equipment includes radar, Decca Navigator, VHF and MF radios, VHF and MF automatic direction finders and echo sounders. The radar scanner has been made watertight so that it will continue to work after the lifeboat has self-righted.

Length: 52ft (15.9m)
Beam: 17ft (5.2m)
Displacement: 32 tons
Load draught aft: 5ft (1.5m)

Left:
Holyhead's 47ft 'Tyne' class doing 18kt. Wales now has seven slipway launching stations equipped with this class of lifeboat.

Above:
Cromer's 47ft 'Tyne' class. With her protected propellers she can be launched down a slipway and can operate in shoal waters and has a top speed of 18kt.

Load draught forward: 3ft 9in (1.1m)
Engines: Twin 460hp diesels
Max speed: 18.5kt
Fuel capacity: 620gal
Range at max speed: 250nm
Crew: 6

33ft (10m) 'Brede' class
With a speed of 20kt this is the fastest of all lifeboats over 10m. Introduced for stations which required something larger than the 'Atlantic 21', yet faster than the 'Waveney' or 'Arun', her GRP hull was developed from a commercial design produced by Lochin Marine of Rye. Before it was adopted for RNLI use the hull was strengthened and a watertight wheelhouse was fitted to make the boat self-righting. Twin diesel engines and a range of electronic and survival equipment completed the transformation of the basic boat into a lifeboat.

The boat has good stability and provides an excellent working platform whether under way or stopped. At the full speed of 20kt the boat lifts to head seas, and spray is thrown clear of the wheelhouse structure; in following and quartering seas it is directionally stable.

The hull is divided into five watertight compartments and void spaces are filled with reserve buoyancy materials. The GRP wheelhouse provides seated accommodation for a crew of four and a stretcher for a casualty. The lifeboat is fitted with VHF radio, an echo sounder, radar and VHF direction finding equipment, all sited within easy reach of the Coxswain. Forward of the wheelhouse is the survivors' cabin which is large enough to take eight seated survivors. Blankets, stretcher, first aid gear and emergency rations are carried.

The boat is fitted with a strong towing bollard and an emergency tiller can be fitted on the port rudder stock. The twin diesel engines are modified to operate after self righting in the event of a capsize and will continue to drive the boat.

Length: 33ft (10m)
Beam: 12ft (3.6m)
Displacement: 8½ tons
Draught: 4ft 3in (1.3m)
Engines: Twin 203hp Caterpillar Type 3208 diesels
Speed: 20kt
Range at max speed: 140nm
Crew: 4

44ft (13.4m) 'Waveney' class
The adaptation of this 44ft design was perhaps the most tangible of the many benefits the RNLI has derived from its membership of the International Lifeboat Federation. At the International Lifeboat Conference held in Edinburgh in 1963 the US Coast Guard presented details of their 44ft cutter and later sent one of the class to the RNLI for evaluation. The result was the first fast (15kt) afloat lifeboat of the RNLI which, with some modifications and additions, became the 44ft 'Waveney' class lifeboat. Today there are 22 of this class in service.

The 'Waveney's hull is divided into seven watertight compartments. The aluminium superstructure is fitted with watertight doors to enclose the cabins, providing additional buoyancy which, combined with the hull design, enables the boat to right in 5sec after a capsize.

The Coxswain is seated in a protected open wheelhouse and seating for the remainder of the crew is in the cabin below. Two cabins forward and aft have space for survivors.

The lifeboat carries a comprehensive range of lifesaving equipment including breeches buoy, scrambling net, stretchers, first aid gear, blankets and emergency rations. Electronic equipment comprises radar, radio telephones, direction finders and echo sounder. An intercom system connects all parts of the boat.

Length: 44ft 10in (13.4m)
Beam: 12ft 8in (3.8m)
Draught: 4ft 2in (1.2m)
Engines: Twin diesels
Speed: 15kt
Radius of action: 95nm
Crew: 5

12m (38ft) 'Mersey' class
The 12m (38ft) 'Mersey' class lifeboat has been designed for stations where the lifeboat has to be launched into the sea from a carriage. There are 22 such stations around the coast.

With a speed of 17½kt, double the speed of the 'Oakley' and 'Rother' class lifeboats she will be replacing, the £350,000 'Mersey' class lifeboat has been designed and developed entirely by RNLI staff, and is the first British lifeboat to be built with an aluminium hull. She is self-righting, has twin 285hp Caterpillar 3208T turbo-charged diesel engines, carries a crew of six and is fitted with the latest communication and navigational equipment.

Three boats of the class are now completed. Two have an aluminium hull and the third is built in fibre reinforced plastic (FRP), another new hull material for the RNLI. They both have the advantage of combining strength with relatively light weight.

50-001

Left:
A huge sea engulfs the sea wall as a 48ft 6in 'Solent' class lifeboat heads out to sea on service at Peterhead in Scotland. There are 10 of the 9kt, steel-hulled 'Solent' class lifeboats still in service with the RNLI, although Peterhead now operates a 47ft 'Tyne'. Aberdeen Journal

Below left:
There are only two of the 50ft 'Thames' class in service, one (photographed here) at Dover and the other at Islay in Scotland.

The FRP-hulled 'Mersey' class is still undergoing extensive trials to evaluate her performance in comparison with the aluminium boats. The two aluminium boats were fitted out at William Osborne's yard at Littlehampton, and the FRP version at Green Marine, Lymington.

Length: 11.57m (38ft)
Beam: 3.81m (12ft 6in)
Depth: 1.86m (6ft)
Draught: 0.875m (2ft 10in)
Displacement: 13 tonnes
Engines: Twin 285hp Caterpillar 3208T turbo-charged marine diesels
Fuel capacity: 1,104 litres (approx 245 gal)
Crew: 6
Speed: 17.5kt maximum
16kt cruising
Range: 180nm at max speed

Displacement Hull Lifeboats

Until the RNLI has completed the introduction of fast lifeboats, it will continue to be admirably served at some stations by the more conventional displacement hull lifeboats. The 'Watsons', 'Oakleys' and 'Rothers' have wooden hulls, the 'Solent' is built in steel. 'Oakleys' self-right using shifting water ballast; 'Watsons', not intrinsically self-righting, are fitted with airbags which automatically inflate to push the lifeboat upright if she capsizes; 'Solents' and 'Rothers' have watertight superstructure which provide a self-righting capability.

While the 'Watsons', 'Solents' and 48ft 6in 'Oakleys' are either launched down slipways or kept permanently afloat, the 'Oakley' and 'Rother' class can be launched by any method, although the 37ft 'Oakley' is nearly always launched from a carriage.

46ft 9in (14.2m)
'Watson' class
Length: 46ft 9in (14.2m)
Beam: 13ft (4m)
Draught: 4ft 4in (1.3m)
Engines: Twin Thornycroft 380s
Speed: Over 8kt
Range at max Speed: 280nm
Crew: 7

48ft 6in (14.8m)
'Solent' class
Length: 48ft 6in (14.8m)
Beam: 14ft (4.3m)
Draught: 4ft 7in (1.4m)
Engines: Twin 110hp diesels
Speed: 9kt
Range at max speed: 240nm
Crew: 7

37ft (11.3m) 'Oakley' class
Length: 37ft (11.3m)
Beam: 11ft 6in (3.5m)
Draught: 3ft 4in (1m)
Displacement, loaded: 13 tons
Engines: Twin 52hp diesels
Max speed:- 8kt
Range at max speed: 140nm
Crew: 7

37ft 6in (11.4m)
'Rother' class
Length: 37ft 6in (11.4)
Beam: 11ft 6in (3.5m)
Draught: 3ft 7in (1.1m)
Displacement, loaded: 13 tons
Engines: Twin 52hp diesels
Range at max speed: 140nm
Crew: 7

Below:
A 47ft 'Tyne' class of the relief fleet *The Famous Grouse*. There are 38 lifeboats over 10m in the relief fleet and these are constantly in use, standing in at stations where the regular lifeboat is away for survey and overhaul.

Famous Lifeboat Designers

Ten lifeboat designers whose work has influenced design trends over the past 200 years.

James Beeching

Winner of the Duke of Northumberland's competition to design a lifeboat in 1851 and the man who inspired the basic lifeboat design which would last for many years. A builder of fishing boats by profession, based at Great Yarmouth, his winning design was a 36ft lifeboat, capable of carrying about 70 people and with a self-righting capability. This was achieved by high end aircases, an iron keel and 2½ tons of water ballast in tanks. A boat built to his design was stationed at Ramsgate and was improved when the water ballast system was exchanged for solid ballast.

Lionel Lukin

Born in Essex in 1742, Lionel Lukin was a coachbuilder who became Master of the Worshipful Company of Coachmakers in 1783. He specialised in humane inventions which included an invalid's bed and a raft for rescuing people who had fallen through ice. In 1785 he patented a design for an 'unimmergible' boat with buoyant gunwales and watertight bulkheads. A Northumberland coble was successfully converted to his design and adopted for use as a lifesaving boat off Bamburgh.

William Wouldhave (below)

The housepainter, teacher of singing and parish clerk from South Shields who was also the disgruntled quasi-winner of the first competition held in 1789 to find the best design for a lifeboat. He was offered (but would not accept) one guinea of the two-guinea prize for his model of a craft which he claimed would 'neither sink, nor go to pieces, nor lie bottom up'. He got the idea, reputedly, from seeing a wooden dish which would not stay upside down floating in a countrywoman's pail of water. *The Shields Gazette*

Henry Greathead

The South Shields boatbuilder who was asked to build a boat incorporating some of William Wouldhave's ideas. The result was *The Original* which appeared in January 1790. Although not self-righting, she was the same both ends, was steered by oar and was given a cambered keel. *The Original* gave 40 years' service at the mouth of the Tyne before being wrecked on rocks, with the loss of two crew members, while rescuing the crew of a brig. Further adaptations of Greathead's original design saw invaluable service in the northeast, not least the *Zetland* (still preserved today), which was on station at Redcar for over 80 years.

Richard Oakley (right)

Principal designer of the RNLI whose 37ft self-righting lifeboat, the 'Oakley' class, entered service in 1958. A larger 48ft 6in version with a cabin was introduced in 1963 and both designs incorporated the innovatory self-righting method of shifting water ballast. One and a half tons of water would transfer into a righting tank on the port side beneath the engines if the lifeboat turned turtle.

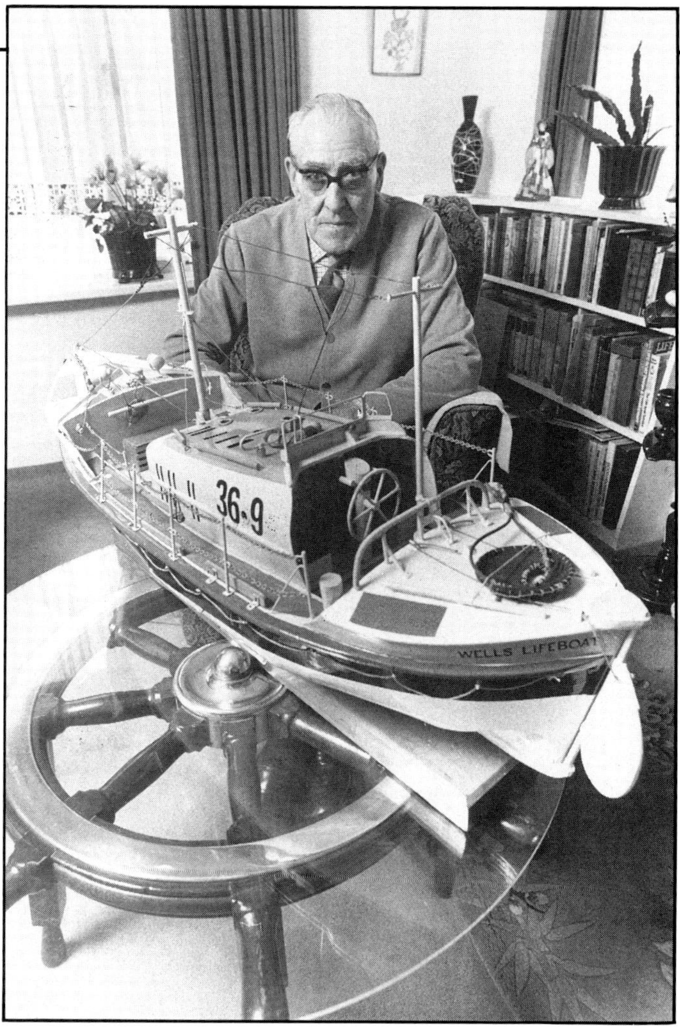

G. L. Watson

G. L. Watson became the RNLI's consulting naval architect in 1887. His influence on design is shown by the fact that there are still 'Watson' class lifeboats in use by the RNLI today. This design was a new lifeboat for Southport following the disaster during the service to the *Mexico* when both St Anne's and Southport lifeboats capsized, killing 27 crewmen. His was the main influence behind the development of steam-driven lifeboats in the late 1800s and, with the advent of the propeller, he designed the familiar protective tunnel in the lifeboat's hull. He was also instrumental in the installation of the first internal combustion engines into lifeboats before his death in 1904.

J. R. Barnett (left)

The man who succeeded G. L. Watson both as head of the Clydeside yacht building firm G. L. Watson & Co, and as the RNLI's consultant naval architect. He held the position until his retirement in 1947 and was involved in lifeboat design for over 60 years. He, like Watson, believed that in larger lifeboats stability rather than a self-righting capability was of overall importance, and it was therefore only when Oakley's new method of self-righting was introduced in the late 1950s that self-righting came back into favour with the RNLI. Barnett-type boats continued to be built up until the early 1960s but the first Barnett boat which incorporated new RNLI-developed 76hp engines was a 60ft twin-screw vessel capable of about 10kt. For the first time two cabins were provided and such was the faith placed in the engines that only a jury rig was provided for emergency sail-powered back-up. *Lafayette*

James Peake

James Peake, Assistant Master Shipwright at HM Dockyard, Woolwich, sat on the original panel judging the Duke of Northumberland's competition of 1851. It was he who was given the task of designing a lifeboat which would incorporate the best features of all the entries submitted. The result was a 30ft boat, both ends alike, steered by oar with cork-filled chambers and no water ballast. Tubes with valves allowed her to free herself of shipped water in 55sec and she took 7sec to self-right. By 1862 there were a hundred 'Peake' lifeboats in service.

Henry Richardson and Henry Thomas Richardson

The father and son team who invented the tubular lifeboat which went on service at Rhyl in 1856 (above). They had been unsuccessful with their design in the 1851 Duke of Northumberland competition but, undeterred, built a version of their boat with two iron tubes divided into watertight compartments, and sailed her from Liverpool to Ramsgate to demonstrate her capabilities. Both Rhyl and New Brighton stations ordered tubular boats and in spite of the exposed position of the crew who rowed from an elevated platform between the tubes, the two stations remained faithful to the design for many years, Rhyl until 1896.

Adm Desmond Hoare

The pioneer of the rigid-hulled inflatable lifeboat whose ideas were incorporated into the RNLI's 'Atlantic 21'. Adm Hoare was headmaster of Atlantic College, St Donats Castle, South Wales, where students operated their own inflatable rescue boat for sailing activities. The application of a rigid hull to an inflatable boat helped to prevent a jack-knifing tendency in the short steep seas of the Bristol Channel and also reduced the boat's drag in the water. Adm Hoare experimented with different length boats until a 21ft version proved ideal. Rigid-hulled inflatables are now used worldwide, and by no means exclusively as lifeboats.

Smugglers and Egg Beaters

HM COASTGUARD AND HELICOPTERS

'This country now possesses the most comprehensive maritime and coastal search and rescue service anywhere outside the United States.' This confident assertion was made by David Mitchell, when he was Parliamentary Under Secretary of State for Transport in an answer to a Commons question about HM Coastguard's 10-year modernisation programme which in 1989 is nearing completion. As well as reflecting his confidence in the Coastguard service, the Under Secretary's statement paid tribute both to the modern efficiency of the RNLI and to the search and rescue work undertaken by the aircraft of the Royal Navy and Royal Air Force.

Coastguards are the co-ordinators of all marine search and rescue operations around our shores. As such they are the first point of contact for any marine emergency, and can be contacted by radio, telex or simply by dialling 999. The Coastguard will take over the planning of any search required, and will liaise with the other rescue services to ensure the most suitable rescue method is used. A typical day can see Coastguards involved in requesting the launch of lifeboats, scrambling helicopters, calling out cliff teams, and always listening out for the next emergency.

The Search and Rescue Helicopters — Colleagues from the Sky

A growing number of today's successful sea rescues are carried out by lifeboats and helicopters working together. The helicopters used for search and rescue (SAR) around our shores are extremely expensive to run and within the United Kingdom it is largely upon the resources of the Ministry of Defence (MOD) that lifeboatmen depend for their airborne colleagues. In the Republic of Ireland the Army Air Corps is responsible for airborne SAR and is co-ordinated through the Marine Rescue Co-ordination Centre at Shannon.

The Royal Air Force and the Royal Navy provide rescue facilities primarily for all military and civilian aircraft in distress within United Kingdom Air Space. Helicopters, however, also provide assistance to any vessel in difficulty within UK waters, and special help in cases of civil distress such as heavy snow, floods, medical emergencies, and cliff or mountain rescues.

Left:
One of HM Coastguard's responsibilities is running cliff rescue teams. Often a rescue of this nature is a co-operative effort between Coastguard and inflatable lifeboat.

Three Coastguard rescue helicopters are operated under contract by Bristows on behalf of the Department of Transport. Two are in the far north of Scotland where the MOD has no military need to station any of its units: one at Sumburgh, Shetlands and the other at Stornoway. The third operates from Lee-on-Solent, Hampshire where the Wessex HU5s of 772 Squadron FAA have been withdrawn and the unit transferred to Portland where it has re-equipped with Sea King HC4s. However, because of the high number of call-outs in the Solent, it was decided that the Coastguard should operate a helicopter on a trial basis.

Rescue Co-ordination Centres

UK Air Space is divided into two SAR regions, each controlled by a Rescue Co-ordination Centre (RCC) fully equipped with extensive communications. The country is roughly divided by a line from the Wash to Anglesey with the northern half's RCC at Pitreavie, near Edinburgh, and the southern at Mount Wise, Plymouth. Each RCC liaises with HM Coastguard's Marine Rescue Co-ordination Centres (MRCC), Air Traffic Control Centres, satellite control centres and various overseas centres, within or on the edges of their coverage. Plymouth, for example, liaises with centres in Canada, America, Ireland, France, Spain and Portugal as well as UK co-ordination centres.

Each centre is manned 24hr a day by a team of RAF personnel. The squadron leader, flight lieutenant and warrant officer are specialists, having made their careers in SAR. Their difficult task is firstly to decide that a helicopter or aircraft is needed and then to co-ordinate and control its use.

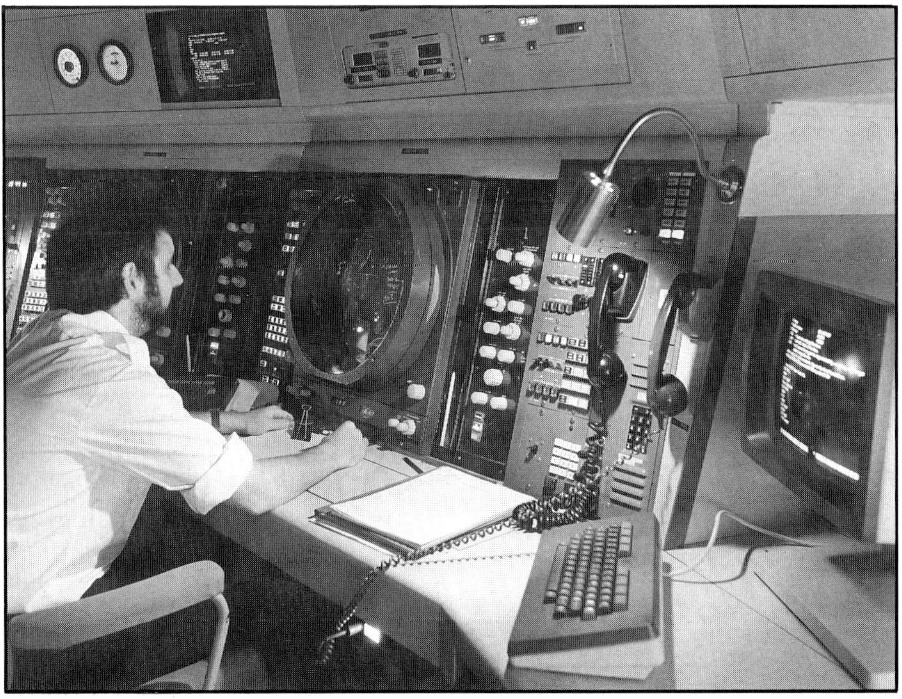

Above:
Some of the equipment used by coastguards of an earlier age exhibited at the Coastguard Museum, Brixham, Devon. It includes rocket line and breeches buoy.

Right:
The density of shipping traffic in the Straits of Dover means concentrated 24hr monitoring by HM Coastguard. In the event of a large scale accident in the Channel, the Coastguard is likely to call upon many lifeboats as well as any or all of the other emergency services. *Crown Copyright*

Right:
A lifeboat's-eye-view of a Royal Navy Sea King winching exercise.
Westland Aircraft Ltd

Sqn Ldr John Murrow, at Plymouth RCC, explains the necessity to question the use of a helicopter in some incidents. Limited resources and high costs mean that a helicopter should only be used in cases of 'immediate life saving', in other words where lives would be endangered or lost without the speed of a helicopter. If other means, such as lifeboat or cliff rescue teams are available and do not add to the risk because of any time delay, then they should be used.

The RCC at Plymouth is also the UK controller of messages from space satellites which detect and locate transmissions from emergency beacons (SAR-SAT/COSPAS). The two satellites transmit every 90min to Toulouse which then passes any messages for Northern Europe to Plymouth which, in turn, either takes necessary action or passes on the information to a relevant centre.

The RCCs have both Sea King and Wessex helicopters at their disposal, as well as one long-range Nimrod aircraft. The Nimrod can also be located at other bases around the UK and is at one hour's readiness both day and night. The Sea Kings can be airborne in a maximum of 15min during the day and 45min at night. Wessex do not normally operate at night because of their limited hover capability but are on 15min readiness during the day. Each station has one helicopter at readiness with another prepared to come to standby if required. Air support is very expensive. The Royal Navy SAR helicopters are funded by the Department of Trade and Industry on a charge basis, each time they are called out to a civilian casualty. Royal Air Force helicopters are budgeted for out of RAF funds.

HM Coastguard — The Lifeboatman's Link with the Shore

Today's high-tech Coastguard service is a long way from the old image of a man with a parrot and a telescope, staring out to sea from a windswept clifftop. It is a highly trained force with all the latest technology from radar to computers, from satellites to VHF direction finders.

The original Coastguard service was set up in 1822 to crack down on smuggling; early coastguards were more interested in saving money for the Revenue than saving lives. However, these early coastguards were also expected to help ships in distress, and in the case of a shipwreck do what they could to save lives, often at the risk of their own. At that time, coastguards frequently provided the crews of early lifeboats and found themselves rowing out into appalling conditions.

The Admiralty retained control of the service until after World War 1, but in 1923 the modern civilian force was born within the Board of Trade. For the first time in its long maritime history Britain had a specialised staff primarily devoted to coastwatching and lifesaving.

HM Coastguard Today

Today's Coastguard service is based on a network of 21 rescue centres spread around the coast, within a framework of six regions. The headquarters for these regions, the Maritime Rescue Co-ordinating Centres (MRCCs), are at Dover, Falmouth, Swansea, Glasgow, Aberdeen and Yarmouth. Within these six regions are between three and five Districts run from Maritime Rescue Sub-Centres. The basis of all SAR co-ordination in the United Kingdom is the constantly staffed watch system at these Centres: 24hr a day, seven days a week, 52 weeks of the year. The heart of the Centres is the Operations Room which is permanently staffed by at least three coastguards maintaining radio, telephone and telex watch. Each Centre is fitted with an Emergency Planning room, press facilities, staff accommodation and storage space for coast rescue equipment and vehicles, usually Land Rovers. All have local radio aerials as well as control of remote aerial sites. They also have the latest communications equipment, quick and efficient communications being the key to modern Coastguard operations. All three international distress frequencies are closely monitored by Coastguards. Developments have included the vital breakthrough of VHF direction finding equipment (VHF DF) which has proved an invaluable tool in locating people in trouble through their VHF signals pin-

Right:
A Royal Navy search and rescue diver from a Wessex HAR 1 helicopter enters the water to assist a downed pilot during training. *Crown Copyright*

Below right:
The busy HM Coastguard Maritime Rescue Co-ordination Centre at Brixham, Devon. Nearly all the calls for help at sea are picked up or relayed through such rescue centres and it is the Coastguard that is usually the first to let a lifeboat station know that its services are required.

pointed between two separate listening posts.

The second major innovation which will have a vital role to play in the foreseeable future is the advent of satellite communications through the International Maritime Satellite (INMARSAT). The UK terminal for maritime distress traffic is at Falmouth MRCC, via Goonhilly Down. This has required Falmouth Coastguard to devise quick and effective methods of communication with other sectors as they will frequently acquire operational information that needs to be acted upon many hundreds of miles away.

Visitors to the Coastguard stand at the London International Boat Show will have seen the unique new system devised by the Coastguard service for marine rescue planning. This deals with the complex problems of arranging the best search patterns and areas, taking into account the different characteristics of the search vessels and aircraft, the prevailing weather, sea conditions and visibility. The computer system calculates the best answer to these problems in a fraction of the time previously taken to arrive at the solution manually. Thus the resources available for a rescue — helicopters, other aircraft, lifeboats and vessels nearby — can be tasked much more quickly and effectively.

The development of satellite communications through Falmouth illustrates the way in which different rescue centres have different specialist responsibilities within the overall network. Aberdeen, for example, has the North Sea oil industry which is estimated to provide 80% of its traffic. At the other end of the country, Dover MRCC has the job of policing a one-way system in the world's busiest shipping lane, the Dover Straits. The Channel Navigation Information Service (CNIS) was introduced in the early 1970s and mid-Channel collisions are now something of a rarity. Liaising with their French counterparts at Cap Gris Nez, Dover transmits regular broadcasts 10 and 40min past the hour on VHF Channel 10, to provide the latest navigation information on activity in the Straits area. Ships are expected to report in on entry to the area from either direction and they must then observe strict regulations on crossing the two one-way traffic flows. The service maintains a spotter aircraft to monitor vessels not complying with the collision regulations, and stiff fines

Above:
A Royal Navy Wessex HU5 from RNAS Culdrose hovers close to a cliff face. *RNAS Culdrose*

can be implemented on rogue ships. Dover and Falmouth are also reporting-in stations for ships with bulk liquid and gas cargoes, or for hampered vessels likely to present a hazard to other traffic using the Strait. The computerised system provides a constantly updated supply of vital information on the position, speed, and course of potential hazards, plus a watching brief on all traffic, just in case.

There is a lot more, of course, to the modern Coastguard than the communications centres, crucial though they are to today's marine rescues. Coastguards also operate coastal searches, cliff, mud and quicksand rescues, provide mobile patrols both ashore, in Land Rovers, and afloat, in general purpose inflatable boats. They also staff Coastguard lookouts at times of bad weather or at similar times of high risk to mariners; and they carry out a vital public relations campaign to put the sea-safety message across to the public, press and media.

There are, however, just 550 regular Coastguards, the rest are the 8,500 Auxiliary Coastguards: men and women with a sense of public duty similar to the crews and fund raisers of the Lifeboat service. Ultimately, of course, everybody on our coasts is an auxiliary coastguard, in that they can all spot an incident and make a 999 call to report it.

Right:
A Sea King HAR3 of the RAF's Sea King Training Flight in action close to the shore. *Ian Allan Library*

Support the Lifeboats!

'A lifeboat service begins from the moment someone drops a coin into the collecting box', said a lifeboat Coxswain. The RNLI, unique amongst the emergency services in the United Kingdom, is supported entirely by voluntary contributions and therefore fund raising supplies the lifeblood of the Institution. Without it the lifeboats would not exist. Why, though, is such a vital rescue service not Government run?

In order to explain this seeming anomaly one must first look back at the original pamphlet published by Sir William Hillary in 1823, in which he proposed an organisation which should be funded by voluntary donations and subscriptions. Obtaining these, he thought, would be 'found easy in its progress and successful in its results'.

However, after the initial enthusiasm for a national lifeboat service the RNLI found itself relying upon the support of a limited number of habitually charitable individuals. By 1854 many lifeboats had become rundown through lack of funds, and the RNLI turned to the Board of Trade for help. The Government agreed to pay a grant of £2,000 a year but with it came restrictions and 'red tape', and in 1869 the RNLI decided that it could and should regain its independence. During the decade following the reorganisation of the 1850s, the Institution received a legacy for £10,000 and the practice was developed of naming lifeboats in accordance with the wishes of those who bequeathed money for the provision of a new boat. Institutions and corporate bodies gave regular help and individual cities began to raise funds. The first inland town to provide a new boat was Ipswich. A letter written on behalf of the clerks, foremen and workmen addressed to their employers, Messrs Ransomes & Sims of Ipswich, stated: 'We believe therefore, that if the claims of this truly excellent Institution were taken up by the principals of similar establishments throughout the kingdom, in the same spirit which we are happy to recognise in you, the result would be such as we should all truly rejoice at.'

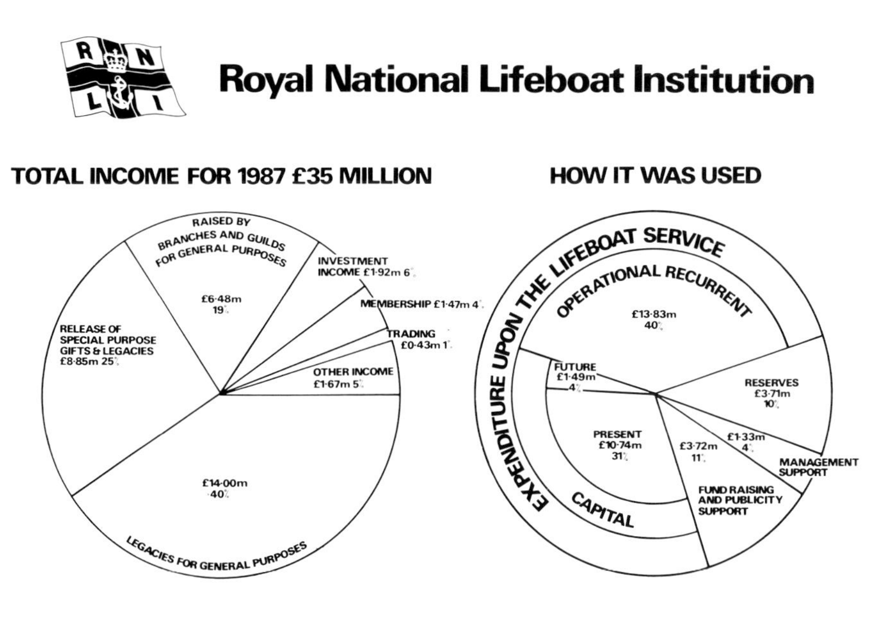

Nevertheless, in the 1880s some two-thirds of the revenue was being provided by only about 100 people and expenditure was exceeding income. A disaster, this time involving two lifeboats, was to set the RNLI on the path to financial success. On 9 December 1886 a German barque, *Mexico*, went aground near Southport in a gale. Southport lifeboat launched but capsized in a heavy sea and only two men from a crew of 15 survived. St Anne's lifeboat, with 14 men on board, launched, and was not seen again until she was found wrecked the next day. Lytham lifeboat launched and rescued the 12 crew from the barque. Twenty-seven lifeboatmen had lost their lives; it was and remains the worst lifeboat disaster.

A relief fund was instituted for the 16 widows and 50 orphans and so successful was this, that a Lancashire businessman, Sir Charles Macara, decided to approach the general public for support for the RNLI itself. On 23 July 1891 he issued an appeal through several newspapers saying that the response to the relief fund had 'emboldened him to appeal once more to the public on behalf of this great national Institution which is sorely in need of funds. This deficit last year assumed alarming proportions and unless the country is roused to supply the necessary means, the Institution's operations will be very seriously curtailed'. The editor of the *Yorkshire Post* took up the cry and in an article asked 'when will the shillings and half-crowns of the gentlemen of England who live at home and at ease, which are so

Left:
The RNLI enjoys the support of many commercial concerns. Lifeboats have been named after grocery chains, whisky brands and oil companies.

urgently needed to pay the mere routine charges, be forthcoming with half the readiness with which these gallant men tender their lives?' The *Yorkshire Post* received £5,500 in 14 days.

Macara's next step, and the most significant of all, was to arrange the very first street collections in Manchester and Salford. A huge procession was held in October 1891 and over £5,000 was raised. This 'Lifeboat Saturday' as it was called was the genesis of flag days. Macara 'brought charity into the streets and the streets into charity'. 'Lifeboat Saturdays' spread nationwide and the Ladies Auxiliary Committee, formed by Lady Macara, began the first collections in private houses, leading to the present house-to-house collections.

Ways of raising money for the RNLI became more diverse and spectacular and through achieving the publicity it needed, the Institution also attracted criticism. Claims were made that the RNLI was wasting money, neglecting the lifeboats and mismanaging its affairs and should be nationalised. So irritating and defamatory were these allegations that the Committee of Management of the Institution were delighted when a select committee was appointed to look into the affairs of the RNLI. The committee held 24 sittings to examine witnesses, and five private sittings. At the end of three months the committee published its report. On every issue the RNLI was vindicated and congratulated on its good management. On the subject of nationalisation the Committee reported: 'We see no ground for recommending that the lifeboat service should be taken over by the state, so long as it is maintained as efficiently and successfully as at present by public benevolence.'

The RNLI has, since 1897, when that report was published, grown to be recognised as one of the top charities in the United Kingdom, in terms of income. Well over £30 million is required each year to run the lifeboat service, with some lifeboats costing over half-a-million pounds each. What is remarkable is that every penny still comes from voluntary contributions.

The RNLI raises its money in a variety of ways, the most reliable being the traditional support from the voluntary fund

Left:
The RNLI was the first charity to bring collecting into the street and gave birth to Flag Days; this photograph shows an early Lifeboat Saturday. The first was organised in Manchester in 1891 and was such a success that similar processions were held in towns throughout the country soon afterwards.

EXAMPLES OF SUCCESSFUL COMMERCIAL LINK-UPS

Birds Eye Foods	*Promotions 1969/70 and 1971:*	On pack. Donation for each pack of fish fingers bought
	Raised Total ***£60,093***:	Lifeboat *Birds Eye* at New Quay, Dyfed
Safeway Food Stores	*Appeal May 1984:*	RNLI chosen for charity month. Fund raising events by staff and customers
	Raised ***£166,328***:	Lifeboat *Safeway* at Calshot, Hants
Newspaper Society	*Appeal 1985:*	Local newspapers carried Appeal and raised money through advertising, donations, fund raising events
	Raised ***£139,655***:	Lifeboat *Newsbuoy* in the Relief Fleet
'Famous Grouse'	*Promotion June-Sept 1986:*	Buy one square of a picture to win a bottle of whisky competition in pubs
	Raised ***£453,003***:	Lifeboat *The Famous Grouse* in the Relief Fleet
Sealink British Ferries	*Appeal 1986:*	Competitions, on pack on duty free goods, donations
	Raised ***£149,914***:	Lifeboat *Sealink Endeavour* at Hastings, Sussex
Beefeater Gin	*Sponsorship 1986:*	30min colour film about the work of the RNLI and Padstow lifeboat *James Burrough*
Volvo Concessionaires Ltd	*Promotion/Sponsorship 1987/88:*	Two-year promotion; raffling Volvo cars in aid of funds; cars at RNLI venues; contact with RNLI members through *The Lifeboat*
	Raised ***£350,000*** *in 1988:*	*Lifeboat Voluntary Worker* for Relief Fleet; Junior membership club 'Storm Force' poster and stickers
British Gas	*Sponsorship 1988:*	Grace Darling 150th Anniversary Appeal funding: advertising, 15min video, colour poster, exhibition travel costs
	Fund Raising:	By staff in aid of the Appeal

raisers. Since the Ladies' Lifeboat Auxiliaries started their work in 1897, just under 2,000 Branches and Guilds of volunteers have been formed. The country is divided up into 13 fund raising regions, each with full-time staff whose job it is to support and encourage the RNLI Branches and Ladies Guilds in their area and to form new Branches wherever possible. Each Branch or Guild carefuly tends its 'patch' and aims to raise more money each year, organising events as diverse as the traditional coffee morning and jumble sale to mammoth raft races and auctions of promises. Events such as these, combined with annual flag days and house-to-house collections, raise one-third of the RNLI's total income each year.

The impact that attending an RNLI event, film and talk may have on an individual is immeasurable but undoubtedly the Branches and Guilds do much work that can never be accredited. That, alongside the publicity which comes from rescues by lifeboatmen, must account for the very high proportion of income as a result of legacies and wills. Over half of the income is raised in this way. The largest legacy ever was £3 million left by a Yorkshire businessman in 1987. No one has been able to trace any link between the generous benefactor and the Lifeboat service, so one can only assume that he was attracted by the heroic work of the lifeboatmen and the good name of the RNLI in general.

Since the 1960s the RNLI's traditional customers, the merchant sailors and fishermen, have been overtaken in numbers by the 'pleasure-craft' users, who now account for over 60% of lifeboat services. In 1969 the RNLI decided to encourage these new customers to become regular subscribers by launching the Yachtsmen's Lifeboat Supporters Association. Round the world yachtsman Sir Alec Rose launched the scheme, saying 'the question which I think we should all now ask ourselves is whether boat owners are doing enough for the RNLI. Some of course are, but it has to be admitted that a good many are not. Now an opportunity is being presented to every man, woman and child who owns a boat or who takes pleasure in going out in boats to give to the Royal National Lifeboat Institution the help it so

Right:
Getting the very young involved: these toddlers are racing in a fun day in aid of the City of Sheffield lifeboat appeal. The day raised £1,400 and the overall appeal for a new lifeboat at Whitby exceeded £450,000. *Sheffield Newspapers Ltd*

badly needs in order to maintain the wonderful volunteer service it has always given.' There were 6,000 members by 1971 and in 1972 the name was changed to 'Shoreline' and was expanded to appeal to all the public. In 1985 a junior membership scheme, 'Storm Force', was introduced with the aim of attracting the interest of young people, possibly potential fund raisers and lifeboat crews, in the work of the lifeboat service. By 1988 there were four levels of adult membership of the RNLI: Life Governor and Governor with voting rights at the RNLI's AGM, and 'Shoreline' individual and joint members; membership totals 128,000. The RNLI not only benefits from a steady flow of subscriptions but good must come from so many people reading *The Lifeboat*, the quarterly journal of the RNLI.

That membership is often attractive to another major source of income, the commercial company. *The Lifeboat* carries advertising and a major company undertaking a promotion in aid of the RNLI can also be assured of reaching some many thousands of people in their target age and income range, by having their support mentioned in the magazine. Approaches are regularly made to major companies for help in terms of one-off donations and for long term support. In return, the connection with a notable charity, the use of that well respected name, enhances the company's product. The 'on-pack promotion' giving a donation for every item bought, or the competition to be entered on collecting so many coupons, have become familiar sights. The RNLI carefully examines every approach and selects those that are appropriate to its image. Similarly the offer of financial help from individuals wishing to carry out sponsored activities which the RNLI considers dangerous, such as high-risk activity without proper safety cover or training, have to be refused.

A notable refusal of money occurred after the defection of former MI5 Chief Guy Burgess to Moscow. He suggested that the four-figure fee which he had been offered by a Sunday newspaper should be given to the RNLI. The Institution declined the money; and the reason for doing so — that the organisation would not be willing to accept money arising from treason — was scarcely open to dispute. What was much to everyone's credit was that, as the result of the way in which the matter was handled by the press, money, exceeding the amount refused, was contributed to the revenue.

The press and media are excellent friends of the RNLI because tales of heroic lifeboat services make good news stories and even better film. However, the media has also raised significant sums of money for the RNLI. BBC's 'Blue Peter' children's programme has held three appeals on behalf of the lifeboats and the latest, in 1984-85, raised sufficient money to buy six inflatable lifeboats. Each is named after the programme and the publicity generated alone must be worth countless thousands of pounds to the RNLI.

Above left:
A modern Lifeboat Saturday: rugby players (and others) pulled a 'D' class inflatable through the streets of Romsey, Hampshire, during Lifeboat Day. The result of the day from a small inland town — £804.40.

Above:
Pubs traditionally help the RNLI. Here the district manager of a rum manufacturer which supports the RNLI helps Aberdeen lifeboat crew break open bottles of coins collected in local pubs for the local lifeboat. *Aberdeen Journals Ltd*

The RNLI's fund raising is alive and well. New schemes, such as the Government's Payroll Giving which began in 1986, are pursued while traditional, tried and tested methods such as Flag Days are not forgotten. Once encouraged to support the lifeboats, benefactors rarely turn away. The Civil Service, Post Office and British Telecom Fund, which started helping in 1870, has now provided 41 lifeboats and is the largest single contributor. Similarly it is not uncommon for wealthy individuals, who have provided a half-million pound lifeboat, which bears their name, to come back some years later and provide another.

Whether it is the multi-international company donation, the lottery ticket, the collected used postage stamps or that single coin in the collecting box, everyone who gives support plays a part in the rescue operation.